THE ACCESSIBLE
HEGEL

THE ACCESSIBLE
HEGEL

MICHAEL ALLEN FOX

Humanity
Books

an imprint of Prometheus Books
59 John Glenn Drive, Amherst, New York 14228-2197

Published 2005 by Humanity Books, an imprint of Prometheus Books

Inquiries should be addressed to
Humanity Books
59 John Glenn Drive
Amherst, New York 14228–2197
VOICE: 716–691–0133, ext. 207
FAX: 716–564–2711

09 08 07 06 05   5 4 3 2 1

Library of Congress Cataloging-in-Publication Data

Fox, Michael Allen, 1940 May 7–
    The accessible Hegel / Michael Allen Fox.
        p. cm.
    Includes bibliographical references and index.
    ISBN 1–59102–258–4 (pbk. : alk. paper)
    1. Hegel, Georg Wilhelm Friedrich, 1770–1831. I. Title.

B2948.F59 2005
193—dc22

2004019442

Printed in the United States of America on acid-free paper

To my sister Robin,
for her support and encouragement over the years,
and for helping to make the world a better place.

And to the memory of
Emil L. Fackenheim (1916–2003),
an extraordinarily learned scholar and wonderful teacher,
whose infectious enthusiasm for Hegel was an inspiration to so many.

CONTENTS

LIST OF ILLUSTRATIONS

ACKNOWLEDGMENTS

T o the many students who have studied Hegel with me, I offer my everlasting thanks. Their questions and insights have certainly taught me more than I can say briefly. However, special thanks goes to Rachel Sheffrin, who read and commented helpfully on early drafts of chapters 1–3. I would like to express my gratitude to Queen's University (Canada) for granting me academic leave in 2003, during which I completed most of the final revisions to this book, and to the School of Social Science, University of New England (Australia), and particularly Fred D'Agostino, then Head of School, for providing me with the space and facilities that enabled me to do so. Anonymous reviewers of my manuscript helped improve it with astute comments, and their time and expertise is much appreciated.

As always, my mate and best friend, Louise Noble, has unfailingly cheered me on and given me new energy and a sense of perspective when I needed them most. I owe her so much.

Hegel is one of the greatest philosophers of all time; by some peoples' reckoning, he would rank first. Certainly his comprehensiveness of outlook and ability to draw diverse and opposing ideas and modes of experience together into a unified rational account of reality are unmatched.

If you are at all like me, your first encounter with Hegel will be somewhat daunting, but you will also learn from it that something in his profound vision of things speaks to your inner self, and you can't let him go after that. The territory he explores—where human activities are shown to be exquisitely rich and full of surprises and deeper meanings—strikes one as strange, yet often oddly familiar. Hegel tells a story that is nothing less than the philosophical history of civilization and what he took to be its most significant accomplishments, in which each participant has had an identity and a role to play. Anyone can therefore profit enormously from reading it.

To say that digesting Hegel's works requires special effort would be a classic understatement. When you begin reading, everything seems rather overwhelming; your head is swimming, and it's hard to get your bearings or to feel sure that you have made any advance. You reread, perhaps, but this helps only a little. Then, after a while, the task gets easier as you persist and press on. Somewhere down the line, things start to fall into place, and you see the overall configuration of his system taking shape. Finally, the details also make sense, and you look back with much improved comprehension and confidence at the texts that had once left you so baffled. What I have described is not an unusual scenario when one attacks a demanding author in any field, and this should be remembered in order to counteract discouragement. My final piece of advice is this: Let Hegel's words wash over you, so to speak, in the justifiable expectation that you *will* understand much better in the end. And, of course, a good volume on Hegel at your side can be of immeasurable service.

I shall not present Hegel with all the rough edges neatly trimmed away; nor shall I set him up in order to dismiss him later on. Those kinds of treatments one finds too readily elsewhere. Rather, I try to make the process of gaining access to Hegel's mindset a little easier without removing the challenge. In order to accomplish this goal, I avoid burdening the reader with coverage of every topic on which he wrote or lectured, and focus instead on showing how to approach Hegel and deal with his style of philosophizing and the unusual concepts and terminology he employs. I concentrate on the major issues that preoccupy him and examine key passages in which these are presented. As a consequence, the reader who subsequently continues to mine Hegel's texts will already have built up a durable framework of understanding. I provide many examples of dialectical thinking for examination, from both Hegelian and non-Hegelian sources. References are also made to other ideas and cultural products that are of general interest. These are intended to stimulate reasoning and the forming of connections that are in the spirit of Hegel. Finally, this book is unique in that original illustrations accompany the text to enhance the reading experience.

My hope is that you will find *The Accessible Hegel* to be a rewarding and entertaining guide and that you will discover how amazing the world looks when viewed from Hegel's quite distinctive standpoint.

1
A NOVEL CONCEPTION OF PHILOSOPHY

THE PROBLEM OF THE STARTING POINT

It is often said that we all philosophize, whether or not we consciously attend to the process. No one will dispute that we can scarcely avoid puzzling our way through concerns about life, the universe, human nature and potentialities, and our responsibilities toward others. Now not everyone wants to *study* philosophy, but everyone, arguably, *has* a philosophy (or perhaps several philosophies). But if someone challenged us with the question, Where (or how) should one begin thinking philosophically? the answer isn't at all obvious. We might start with some indisputable (axiomatic or "foundational") truths, if we thought there were any. Or we might begin with everyday experience of the world, or inner experience of our own mental states and emotions, and reflect on that. We might explore and debate the ideas of others who have philosophized before us. We could also look closely at our language to discover what interesting perspectives it contains and what directions it suggests to our thinking. All of these approaches have been tried, plus many others, and there is no universal agreement on the "correct" way to proceed. Each pathway into philosophy depends on certain underlying assumptions about what is to be taken as a starting point. But what if we made *no* such assumptions? Would all of our inquiries then be devoured by skeptical doubts and come to naught?

Georg Wilhelm Friedrich Hegel (1770–1831) did not think so. His response—a refreshing and invigorating one—was that it matters little where we start or whether we assume anything; our philosophical journey will inevitably be a prolonged process of self-examination in which thought interrogates itself and remedies its deficiencies as it progresses. The end result at which we arrive "justifies" the starting point we have chosen by proving its fruitfulness for yielding knowledge. This paradoxical-sounding hypothesis furnishes an important key to revealing the secret of Hegel. Before we investigate his position further, however, it will be helpful to set Hegel within the historical context that influenced him. It is also faithful to Hegel's own commitments, with respect to how we ought to view thinkers of the past, that we should start out this way.

Hegel's philosophical milieu was one that featured thoroughgoing reassessments of the underpinnings of thought and culture. His historical period was defined to a large extent by the rise of modern science, ongoing debates over the status of religion, Enlightenment-inspired ideals of human progress and perfectibility, the egalitarian inspiration of the American and French Revolutions, colonialism, and the great creative energy of the Romantic movement in the arts. (Beethoven, Wordsworth, and Hegel were all born in the same year.) These ideas, tendencies, events, and sources of inspiration filtered into his philosophy, which became suffused with their influence. Situated in the era that he was, Hegel inherited an important philosophical legacy: the practice, indeed the requirement, of making a fresh beginning in matters of knowledge and understanding. His conception of philosophy, accordingly, was strikingly different from that of his contemporaries and indeed from that of most practitioners of the art who have come after him.

The philosophical momentum in which Hegel was caught up had been building in strength since the Renaissance, specifically since the time of René Descartes (1596–1650). Descartes had distinguished himself in the minds of many as "the first modern philosopher" by his self-imposed imperative to take for granted nothing that previous philosophers or authorities had said, to accept no beliefs as certain and incorrigible, and to treat philosophical method itself as a challenging and ultimate philosophical problem.

Descartes thus set the agenda for the canonical great thinkers of the seventeenth and eighteenth centuries: Baruch Spinoza, Gottfried von Leibniz, John Locke, George Berkeley, David Hume, and Immanuel Kant. Each of these figures self-consciously broke new ground in the area of philosophical method, and all began their investigations by working through questions about the nature, scope, and boundaries of human knowledge and conscious awareness. Hegel worked under this same potent influence. In the very first main section of his *Encyclopedia of the Philosophical Sciences* (first published in 1817), he wrote: "Philosophy misses an advantage enjoyed by the other sciences. It cannot like them rest the existence of its objects on the natural admissions of consciousness, nor can it assume that its method of cognition, either for starting or for continuing, is one already accepted."[1] Here it is apparent that Hegel was preoccupied from the outset by the need to reexamine critically the point of departure and method of inquiry in philosophy, and his position in the history of Western thought is inseparable from this issue. Apart from this fact, however, it should be noted that the above observation concerning philosophy holds equally true today: Every definition of the discipline embodies a perspective on how one ought to do philosophy—a particular conception of the agenda to be pursued and of how one should go about this.

PHILOSOPHY'S HISTORICAL CONTINUITY

What has been outlined thus far, however, does not yet touch upon the uniqueness and ingenuity of Hegel's approach to philosophy and philosophical problems. To begin with, he not only examined the foundations of thought and culture in every major respect but also claimed to have discerned a pattern or progression in the evolution of philosophical thought itself toward an ever-increasing and more unified comprehension of human reality and the natural world. He held, further, that anyone who grasped this total development in all its essentials must necessarily conceive of the history of philosophy as an organic process in which the contributions of those who helped shape it converge toward the common goal (albeit dimly perceived or even altogether unknown to them) of universal enlightenment. Half a century later, Friedrich Nietzsche (1844–1900) would argue that the history of philosophy represents nothing more than a series of egoistic and idiosyncratic attempts to gain personal power and some measure of control over the universe by imposing ideas on it, each thinker aspiring to be hailed as the "'unriddler of the universe.'"[2] As we shall see (in chapter 6), Hegel was no stranger to the notion that human passions often serve a higher purpose, unbeknownst to us. Nevertheless, he always insisted that whatever the passing parade of appearances and personal agendas might suggest, the study of philosophy, properly conceived, does not present us with a meaningless clash between competing worldviews. Rather, it reveals a body of knowledge that is an integrated whole, comprising numerous limited approaches to the true nature of reality, each woven into a single fabric. This insight indelibly stamped Hegel's philosophical method, both as a natural outgrowth of tendencies discoverable in the work of past philosophers and as an attempt to unite these and give them their most mature, complete expression—a theme we shall explore later on in more detail.

Precisely because he viewed philosophy as having a history, and the history of philosophy as an encompassing process of the sort just described, Hegel could regard his own philosophical system as the drawing together and fulfillment of all those that went before. Thus his "new" beginning or "original" starting point is in a sense both old and new. It is old in that Hegel saw himself as continuing a lengthy tradition of inquiry that has a coherent story to tell and a definite direction of movement. But it is new in the respect that Hegel (so he contended) was the first philosopher who self-consciously understood the total development in which he himself took part. And by virtue of that same awareness, he then became able to carry this universal philosophical project to its conclusion. As he observes, "In philosophy the latest birth of time is the result of all the systems that have preceded it, and must include their principles; and so, if, on other grounds, it deserve the title of philosophy, [it] will be the fullest, most comprehensive, and most adequate system of all."[3]

We can immediately see, against the background of this theoretical assumption, that the way in which Hegel positioned his own achievement does not merely amount to an act of vain and arrogant boasting. On the contrary, his assertion that his own philosophy was the culmination of the history of philosophy is but the logical consequence of his theory, just as his own philosophical achievement represents the logical outcome of attempting to demonstrate the truth of that theory. We can look at Hegel's claim in a slightly different manner too. Imagine that you are a serious philosopher. Suppose further that you believe the history of philosophy exhibits many and diverse endeavors to comprehend human reality and the natural world adequately. You may then view your own philosophical contribution as simply another outlook, a "corrective," perhaps, to all of the false or limited outlooks of your predecessors. This would reflect the standard, "adversarial" notion of the relationship between philosophical positions.[4] A second way of appraising your own effort, however, would be as an attempt to build upon the thought of others in a constructive and supportive spirit. Yet a third way would be to see your philosophical contribution in a quite different light, namely, as a thoroughgoing demonstration that the history of philosophy is something far more than a sundry collection of incompatible, warring worldviews, each jockeying for a superior competitive position, and also as much more than a dialogue of the ages, or even a cooperative enterprise. This "something far more" that you have discovered is the idea of philosophy as a single movement through time toward some discernible end-state. Having adopted such a conception, it would then be natural to attempt, in your own thought construction, to bring about a reconciliation of, and a move beyond, those opposing elements of the various philosophies that constitute the intellectual heritage upon which you are building.

THE SELF-DETERMINATION AND SELF-VINDICATION OF THOUGHT

Hegel did indeed view his philosophical project in this overarching way. His conception of philosophy combines a desire to allow speculative thought to evolve, according to its own natural rhythm, principles, and speed, with a determination to escape from the restrictions and the overemphases, the timidity and the excesses, of past thinkers. Because he conceived of philosophy in this holistic mode, Hegel also believed that with the completion of his system he had, in some important sense, written the final chapter in the history of philosophy. For he firmly held that he'd refined a method whereby thought could overcome all the barriers against which it had struggled since the time of Thales of Miletus (fl. c. 580 BCE), the earliest Western (pre-Socratic) philosopher on record. This method, which we shall investigate later, would afford thought the unrestricted freedom and impetus to reach its goal. Hegel further proposed that thought itself would be the judge as to when this finishing point has been reached. Such a claim may strike us as circular (assuming the very point at issue), hence vacuous, with thought lifting itself up by its own bootstraps. Yet as Hegel himself realized full well and often remarked, this is the way in which all "scientific" (meaning organized and methodical) knowledge is accumulated: It is disciplined, reflective thought that defines the task of inquiry, poses specific problems, refines the method of investigation, and determines when adequate answers have been attained. In line with this idea, Hegel believed he had, through his own efforts, made the philosophical enterprise self-conscious by his very act of becoming aware of its age-old strivings as the natural movement of thought, positing and ever revising its own limits and criteria of success. Thought, at this level of advancement, assesses its achievements and shortcomings in the very act of either securing its goals or falling short of them. But so has it always done, as he was now the first to grasp. Hegel's optimistic credo was that we can trust the ultimate deliverances of consciousness concerning itself, resulting from its own self-critique. Thus, rational and reflective cognition should be viewed as self-corrective—as self-improving, self-transcending, and always capable of moving beyond its own conclusions when defect is discovered therein by thought's activity itself. In this manner, the paradox that thought is the arbiter of its own achievements is allayed, to some extent at least.

Now one could take the claim I have just been discussing as nothing more than an elaboration of what we all readily grasp: that human consciousness is self-aware, reflexively self-critical, and continuously self-revising. And Hegel does affirm these beliefs in an attempt to "normalize" philosophy—especially his philosophy—by bringing it into line with common sense, folk wisdom, and everyday life. As he observes, "everything human is human because it is brought about through thinking, and for that reason alone."[5] But Hegel's position on the nature of philosophy was far more complex than this would seem to indicate. For he remarks that "philosophy is a peculiar mode of thinking—a mode by which thinking becomes cognition, and conceptually comprehensive cognition at that."[6] Philosophy, in other words, seeks fullness of understanding in a way all its own, and its success as a discipline must therefore be assessed according to special standards. We shall come to appreciate how it is that these standards, as Hegel claims, are discovered and set by philosophical thought itself.

Furthermore, Hegel believed that thought cannot really draw fixed limits to its own ability to advance into the unknown, as his important immediate predecessor, Immanuel Kant (1724–1804), had argued. Why not? The answer is that conceptualizing such boundaries necessitates apprehending them *as* boundaries, which, in turn, requires the realization that some space, horizon, or clearing lies beyond. Just as a physical boundary (e.g., a wall) has an inside, so too does it possess an outside, which is part of our awareness of it as a wall in cognition, language, and imagination. And this "outside" is a function of the openness extending away from it. But thought should be conceived of in an analogous manner, Hegel declares. It follows that in the mind, as much as in the physical world, there's at least the possibility that barriers may not pose ultimate limits, since we already overleap them in thought by the very act of thinking about them: "No one knows, or even feels, that anything is a limit or defect, until he is at the same time above and beyond it."[7] If we have access to both sides of a barrier in the manner Hegel suggests, then in some important sense what seemed to be a limit ceases being one at all. He uses pain to illustrate his point. We can think our way beyond a painful state that we are in because we are creatures with a "universal vitality" that projects itself temporally on both sides of the present moment. Hence we can adopt a perspective that overcomes the burdensome immediate sensation. As Hegel affirms, "Consciousness . . . is something that goes beyond limits, and since these limits are its own, it is something that goes beyond itself."[8] The drawing below may help crystallize the argument we have just been examining.

No windows = no experience of outside world.

"Stone walls do not a prison make, Nor iron bars a cage. . . ."[9]

Limits . . . and beyond.

Perhaps, then, observes Hegel, there is an open vista for thought such that human intelligence can, in principle, override all of its self-imposed limits. If so, the argument goes, then there is hope that it may be able to conceptually assimilate all of reality.

After discussing the notion of a limit in general, Hegel adds: "A very little consideration might show that to call a thing finite or limited proves by implication the very presence of the infinite and unlimited, and that our knowledge of a limit can only be when the unlimited is *on this side* in consciousness."[10] This suggests two things: (a) we *are* capable of knowing reality, and (b) that which is ultimately to be known somehow lies nascent within us *already* in some form. More specifically, these propositions entail (1) that thought is by its very nature aligned with the inherent rational principle of the universe (i.e., the *Logos* in which the ancients believed) and (2) that in the final analysis, thought will find itself in harmony with things and will discover in the world its true home and resting place. We see these ideas presented in the following text excerpt: "The real nature of the object is brought to light in reflection; but it is no less true that this exertion of thought is *my* act. If this be so, the real nature [of objects] is a *product* of *my* mind, in its character of thinking subject . . . removed from extraneous influences."[11] In short, *the world as we come to know it is the world that stands before the eye of thought.* It makes no sense to speak of the world as it is "in itself," apart from the inquiring consciousness, for every act of knowing is a "taking in" and "fashioning" by the mind. Hence, being part of the contents of consciousness, the world will exhibit itself truthfully insofar as thought interrogates it and, testing its concepts against experience, establishes the way things actually are. We see here that thought always adopts a stance directly or indirectly in relation to experience, and so Hegel's views never come as "news from nowhere."[12]

A radical theory of this sort cannot be dogmatically laid down, nor assumed to be true, as Hegel was well aware. Hence he asserted that only his *entire system* could be held to vindicate it. With the twenty-two projected volumes that will compose the most complete edition of Hegel's works, there has never been another philosopher who has dared ask so much of readers by way of patience, diligence, devotion, and sheer intestinal fortitude.[13] One hardly needs encouragement to wonder that so few have traveled the entire route in order to discover for themselves whether Hegel's estimate of his own place in the history of philosophy is warranted, exaggerated, or falsified. Nevertheless, we must, at least provisionally, grant him the benefit of the doubt on this matter, momentous as it is, in that he is only telling us, candidly and without evasion, that the fruit of his philosophical labors will justify (if anything can) his starting point and general orientation. ("The proof of the pudding is in the eating," as we say.) Clearly, Hegel's personal objective was to comprehend all of reality philosophically, or as he likes to put it, "thinkingly." This, then, is the reason why we are presented with nothing less than his collected works, dealing with all aspects of human life and experience, as a self-supporting thought-product.

It was also a tenet of Hegel's philosophizing that the dimensions of human activity and consciousness toward which he turned his attention were inseparably interrelated and correlated. Art, religion, history, social morality, political institutions, science, and philosophy itself were all grist for his mill and must be investigated in order to probe exhaustively the nature of reality. Hegel asserts, as we have observed, that one can begin with any feature of human experience that poses a philosophical problem (e.g., the nature of sense-experience, of beauty, of goodness, of reality, or of God) and one will then find one's initial inquiry rippling outward steadily until, sooner or later, all of these areas are implicated and compel our examination. Here, he is once again drawing our attention to the tendency of thought to seek totality of understanding, to form progressively comprehensive links and integrations between its objects and among the concepts by means of which we sort through our experience of, and thought about, the world.

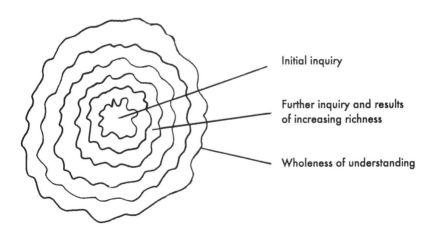

Initial inquiry

Further inquiry and results of increasing richness

Wholeness of understanding

Expanding domains of thought.

Some extraordinary assertions are put forward in framing this approach, to be sure, but they are perhaps not so foreign as may at first seem to be the case. Anyone who has studied philosophy carefully will have learned the lesson that pondering issues in aesthetics, philosophy of religion, philosophy of history, philosophy of science, or ethics, for example, inevitably leads to a confrontation with basic epistemological questions concerning the sources and reliability of knowledge claims, the difference between knowledge and belief, verification, and similar matters, or with basic metaphysical questions about the nature of a person, whether we have free will, whether there is purpose in nature, and so on. In addition, as Hegel observed, adequate understanding of a historical epoch, dominated by a vital, powerful, and culturally enriched society (such as that of ancient Athens), calls for insight into that society's many achievements in the arts, humanities, sciences, and every other field, which are interwoven so as to create its singular character and explain its significance and impact upon the world.

Hegel held a still more exalted opinion of philosophy than has so far been indicated, however. In his mature writings, he placed philosophy at the pinnacle of human achievement. The reasons why he did so may have begun to emerge but will become clearer only after we have examined his metaphysics in chapters 3 and 4. However, in general, it may be said that philosophy occupies the lofty summit of endeavor because it is a sort of "superscience" of retrospective assimilation, a way of comprehending that surpasses all others in scope and penetration, overreaching and subsuming every important realm of human activity as well as every other knowledge-seeking discipline. Philosophy interprets all of these subject matters, "purifying" their content in two ways. First of all, philosophy allows insight to become articulate, in the rational mode of language.[14] Thus, the emotive, pictorial, and imagistic representations of art and religion are supplanted by a more sober form of discourse, that of discursive philosophical argument. Second, philosophy strives to render this content in a conceptually adequate fashion, that is, in a way that stands up to the rigorous self-scrutiny of thought. Because philosophy provides an intellectual or cognitive framework for discerning the pattern of development in all spheres of human activity, Hegel thinks, it can be designated as the truest source of understanding of the world and of our own species, whose existence is essentially rooted in the world. Philosophical knowledge, in short, embraces all the things that men and women do or have ever done to try to represent or genuinely fathom the nature of things (art, religion, science, metaphysics), to work out a system or code for living (ethics, politics, law), and to struggle for group self-expression and ascendancy (history). Authentic philosophers, according to Hegel, understand all of these things and understand *that* they understand. Their knowledge may therefore be called "absolute" because it transcends the limitations imposed on thought by every previous approach to discerning the nature of reality. It does so by recognizing them as inhibited, partial, and merely perspectival, then self-consciously correcting their defects, and in doing so, passing beyond these. But philosophy should not only comprehend its subject matter, it must in addition recognize itself simultaneously as doing so. In order to perform this complex, multileveled task, philosophy, as we shall see, forges its own conceptual tools while it progresses, learning about their effectiveness and validating them in the process of evolving and utilizing them.

HEGEL'S METAPHILOSOPHY

A few summary observations may now be made about Hegel's theory of philosophy (or "metaphilosophy"). First, as I have explained above, *philosophy is historical.* It does not just have a history in some fortuitous, merely chronological sense; rather, it is properly considered as historically constituted in a very profound sense. Every philosophy has its time and place, its context not only of ideas but also of events. It is spatially, temporally, and culturally situated and cannot properly be understood in isolation from this context. Concerning the discipline as a whole, Hegel offers the following appraisal: "We may either say, that it is one philosophy at different degrees of maturity: or that the particular principle, which is the groundwork of each system, is but a branch of one and the same universe of thought."[15] This passage gives evidence of Hegel's historicism as well as of his notion that thought is inevitably self-transcending and systematic. Each philosophical construction gives voice to a perspective (a "particular principle") that seems truthful to its author, living at the time and place it is recorded. Hence, every outlook must be understood as a standpoint that arises from within a particular sociocultural context, and against such a background, we see that it is not refuted by later developments but rather supplanted by a succession of views each of which seemed more truthful to *its* author, situated in a *different* time and/or place. Interpretation of this sort, involving, as it does, historicist and social constructionist principles, has proved enormously influential ever since Hegel's works first appeared.[16] But in spite of this commitment to historicism, Hegel also holds, as we see here, that the truth being aimed at is disclosed, in some characteristic but only partial fashion, by each comprehensive philosophical approach.

We can glean an additional lesson about thought itself from the passage just quoted—that the results of thought are always its emergent creations. That is, the forward movement inherent in the cognitive processes that Hegel wishes to describe in his philosophy is one in which new conceptions, theories, and so forth, which were never before entertained, spring forth as if by magic. But, of course, the "magic" here is only apparent; the origin of concepts can be traced to the fluid, germinating process whereby thought posits, then negates and transcends, its own prior conclusions. In chapters 2 and 3, we will examine how this works in some detail.

Hegel demonstrated in very strong terms that studying the history of philosophy is a prerequisite for anyone who would make an original contribution to the discipline. But he also insisted that in order to acquire an accurate comprehension of a past philosopher, one must attempt to rethink or "reenact" his or her ideas. In other words, one must adopt the role of a scholarly apprentice so as to appreciate the dominant intellectual and cultural trends of the times, what features of humans or the world presented themselves to the thinker as posing an irresistible philosophical challenge, how he or she reacted to this challenge as a philosopher, whether the thought-system produced was internally consistent and really achieved its goals, and how the given standpoint posed problems for those who followed and who perceived *it* as an irresistible challenge. Hegel's main principle of assessment was that in reflecting on the work of past philosophers, all criticism must be *internal* or *contextual*. That is, it must be predicated on the kind of close study outlined above and aimed at disclosing the core of the philosopher's position. It is easy to extrapolate from this idea to Hegel's broader conception of the entire history of philosophy as an indivisible whole, the central significance of which must be grasped by, and embraced within, his own system of thought.

He states his position even more boldly in a passage in his *Lectures on the History of Philosophy*:

[E]very philosophy has been and still is necessary. Thus none have passed away, but all are affirmatively contained as elements in a whole. But we must distinguish between the particular principle of these philosophies as particular, and the realization of this principle throughout the whole compass of the world. The principles are retained, the most recent philosophy being the result of all preceding, and hence no philosophy has ever been refuted. What has been refuted is not the principle of this philosophy, but merely the fact that this principle should be considered final and absolute in character.[17]

Here, we are told that not only does each historical contribution to philosophy have its logical place in the total layout of the discipline but also it is an indispensable constituent thereof and an active presence therein. Its pretensions to authoritativeness may have melted away, but its dynamic energy remains a palpable force in the world of ideas. This explains why today's thinkers continue to comb through the writings of their predecessors, unendingly seeking after, and unearthing, new insights.

Against this background, we can also explain two additional observations Hegel makes about philosophy. One is that "the history of philosophy is identical with the system of philosophy."[18] There is, of course, a double meaning here: (1) the history of philosophy is a single system, and (2) its essence or truth is expressed in Hegel's own system. We'll focus on the second meaning for a moment. Simply put, it is that his own contribution is to be understood as that of assimilating the history of philosophy, expressing its inner principle of advance, and completing its evolution. His project would then appear to be the last act in this drama, or at least the beginning of the end.

Hegel's other general observation is paradoxical: "that [in plumbing the history of philosophy] we are *not dealing with what is past* but rather with actual thinking, with our own spirit."[19] By this he wishes to convey that the past is alive in the present; the same perennial philosophy is still energized and is still being worked out. Thus, so far as philosophy is concerned, the past both is and is not over and done with. Those who thought and wrote previously are dead and their viewpoints are fixed in time, but their ideas flow on as influences, both overt and concealed. We could say that they are dissolved in the tide of knowledge with which today's thought merges.

The second major metaphilosophical idea of Hegel's is that *truth in philosophy is a matter of coherence*, or of how well and to what extent different beliefs interlock and coalesce into an organized theoretical structure. It would be a mistake to assume that this entails that every item of knowledge, however trivial, has endless ramifications, as one common caricature of Hegel's view suggests. I shall examine the notion of coherence in chapter 5, but for now it need only be noted that it is much closer to Hegel's intent to say that truth is a function of embeddedness within a system or matrix of ideas. Truth may be gauged according to different levels of attainment, but it is also to be conceived of as a process, not as a fixed thing or mere result.

Hegel's third broad claim is that *philosophy is circular*. This has several meanings, which we need to probe. For one thing, philosophical thought can use any item of experience as a springboard or jumping-off point. Because philosophical issues overlap and merge into one another's conceptual territory, as indicated earlier, each branch of the subject can be investigated in its own right; as well, each eventually propels the inquirer onward into every other. The deeper explanation of this movement is that every area of philosophy expresses the same emerging truth in its own particular guise. If reality is a rational whole, then this key insight will ultimately be expressed by thought, whether the particular topic it is preoccupied with is ethics, politics, history, art, religion, or any other to which philosophy has traditionally turned its attention. Finally, Hegel wishes to persuade us that no matter where we commence philosophizing, our long and arduous voyage to a final terminus will vindicate our modest point of departure by expressing and maturing the germ of truth it contained unawares. Hegel summarizes this very complex set of ideas:

> Each of the parts of philosophy is a philosophical whole, a circle rounded and complete in itself. In each of these parts, however, the philosophical Idea [roughly, the ultimate result, the truth] is found in a particular specificality or medium. The single circle, because it is a real totality, bursts through the limits imposed by its special medium, and gives rise to a wider circle. The whole of philosophy in this way resembles a circle of circles. The Idea appears in each single circle, but, at the same time, the whole Idea is constituted by the system of these particular phases, and each is a necessary member of the organization.[20]

So philosophy is like a cluster of soap bubbles that feed off each other and remain distinct while at the same time having the propensity to merge into a single big structure.

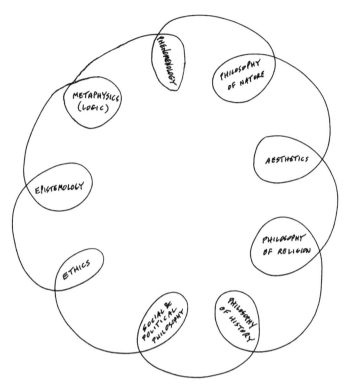

The interlinked circles of philosophy.[21]

One may equally well regard the discipline of philosophy as a unified, organized body of knowledge or as a whole that comprises several inter-linked parts. Shortly after the passage just cited, Hegel continues exploiting the circle metaphor, applying it to the initial entry into philosophy:

> It is by the free act of thought that it occupies a point of view, in which it is for its own self, and thus gives itself an object of its own produc-tion. Nor is this all. The very point of view, which originally is taken on its own evidence only, must in the course of the science be con-verted to a result—the ultimate result in which philosophy returns into itself and reaches the point with which it began. In this manner philosophy exhibits the appearance of a circle which closes with itself, and has no beginning in the same way as the other sciences have. To speak of a beginning of philosophy has a meaning only in relation to a person who proposes to commence the study, and not in relation to the science as science.[22]

In brief, every beginning is provisional, but by being transformed through a painstaking process into a result, it can be shown not to have been so arbitrary as at first it appeared. Indeed, we learn that it had not been arbitrary at all because the final insight was "extracted" from it, as metal is from ore. Alpha and Omega are fused into one; the snake's head swallows its own tail.

Even if the imagery here is powerful, this "circularity" claim will strike some as more than a little dubious. For how can there be a "beginningless beginning" to philosophy (or anything else)? As Søren Kierkegaard (1813–1855) observed, "a logical system must not boast of an absolute beginning, because such a beginning is just like pure being, a pure chimera. . . . How do I bring to a halt the reflection set in motion in order to reach that beginning?"[23] And isn't a self-supporting system of ideas merely a fiction anyway? How can it make contact with reality? To offset the suspicion that some shady business is going on here, consider the following analogy. A language such as English, according to many specialists, is a closed system of just the sort that Hegel describes—a system that feeds off itself. Known as the "holistic theory of meaning" (or "semantic holism"), this view reflects the fact that every term in English (for example) is definable by other terms in the language, and these, in turn, by still others, none of which stands on its own. The entire system goes back and forth, round and round, each element being implicated definitionally by others, and vice versa. The system is endlessly self-referential and, as it were, hangs by its own skyhook. More generally, "the meaning of a symbol is relative to the entire system of representations containing it. Thus, a linguistic expression can have meaning only in the context of a language."[24] Is there an entry point? What makes it all work? How do children ever learn a language? Where does language make contact with the world? These questions are much debated, but we needn't be sidetracked by them here. Suffice it to say that they pose the same challenges that Hegel's theory of philosophy must face. The point I am after is not that Hegel's view becomes any less controversial by being compared with an equally controversial contemporary theory of language, only that it deserves to be taken with like seriousness and not dismissed out of hand.

Another analogy is supplied by music. Consider a theme and a set of variations on it, such as Bach's *Goldberg Variations*, Beethoven's *Diabelli Variations*, or Brahms's *Haydn Variations*. Here we have a simple initial musical statement that is followed by an increasingly elaborate series of embellishments that continually mine the original theme, drawing out its potential or expressing its "truth," as Hegel might say. But although they do so, they are governed in an important sense by that theme and hence never fully transcend or abandon it. They keep returning to it so that the whole that expands outward from it is a "circle of circles" of growing enrichment. The "circularity" of Hegel's philosophy is a fascinating topic on which much has been written.[25] We will take it up again in chapter 3.

IDEALISM PLUS EMPIRICISM

One more point of importance requires emphasis here. For Hegel, philosophy does not just start anywhere and then shoot off into the hyperspace of imaginative fancy, settling back to earth finally at some arbitrary and wholly mysterious and distant time and place. In fact, as we shall see (in chapter 4), this is precisely the extravagance with which Hegel charged a number of his Romantically inspired contemporaries and to which he vehemently contrasted his own approach. Despite what his many noteworthy detractors, from Kierkegaard and Karl Marx to Karl Popper and A. J. Ayer, have alleged, he does not leave experience behind and remains ever faithful to the world. He most emphatically does not deny or doubt the existence of the physical world, to which, he takes it for granted, we are intimately connected. Indeed, it is the philosophers who deem it appropriate to speak of "the external world" that are more likely to wind up in skeptical denial of this sort. Hegel is an *idealist*, to be sure, in the technical sense that he regards the activity of mind or spirit as primary in the scheme of things and as formative in knowledge-gathering activities.[26] Thought, he asserts, is our "highest and most inward life," our "innermost self," whose "cravings" we must "gratify."[27] He also argues, as we have seen, that "The real nature of the object is . . . a *product* of *my* mind." In saying this, Hegel does not mean to suggest that thought simply *invents* a world but rather that rational reflection is responsible for the refinements that clarify how the nature of things is to be understood.

While he holds a sober and considered view of idealism and its merits as a theoretical approach to epistemological and metaphysical problems, Hegel can't resist indulging in curious metaphors in order to amplify his position. For instance, he tells us that "thinking is in fact essentially the negation of something immediately given—just as we owe our eating to food because without it we could not eat. It is true that, in this context, eating is represented as ungrateful, since it is the digesting of that to which it is supposed to owe itself. In this sense, thinking is no less ungrateful."[28] Notwithstanding this sort of amusing eccentricity, Hegel maintains a respectful, even deferential, attitude toward experience and what the world has to teach us.

Thought has its own characteristic properties: it is *self-identical* (a seamless continuum), *reflexive* (self-aware), *fallible* (prone to error), and *self-transcending* (progressively self-improving). But cognition is not a rarefied world unto itself. Just as experience is infused with thought's contribution, or, as we might say, is constructed by thought, so too is our cognitive life saturated with sensory input and continually engaged in testing its constructions by reference to experience. As Hegel states, "experience is the real author of *growth* and *advance* in philosophy."[29] It follows that Hegel is far from being the dour "abstract" thinker he is often superficially made out to be, with concerns entirely remote from ordinary life and everyday awareness. On the contrary, he is, as he would himself state, "concrete" in his dedication to gathering up the strands of experience in order to make sense of them in a unified way. This shows that he has assimilated and incorporated the lessons of the empiricist tradition into his outlook on an equal footing with those of the rationalist tradition.

THE TRANSCENDENCE OF HEGEL?

I shall not attempt to reach a definitive verdict on the success of Hegel's philosophical project in this book. Suffice it to say that the subsequent history of philosophy has been one of decreasing faith in universal rationality and of increasingly constricted views of the nature of philosophy and its methodolgy. Grandiose visions such as Hegel's have therefore fallen into disrepute, though strong interest remains in many aspects of his thought, which numerous thinkers have appropriated in one way or another. However, even his most ardent admirers have noticed a peculiarity concerning the endurance of his philosophical contribution, and we might dwell on it for a moment. Simply put, many students of Hegel have wondered whether, on purely Hegelian grounds, his own philosophy was fated to become superseded by another thought-formation. For if, according to Hegel, philosophy is to be understood as a knowing and deliberate absorption of its own past achievements that brings to fulfilment a common rational purpose inherent in them, then shouldn't the next step beyond Hegel amount to an assimilation of *his* thought into a picture of reality that is *still more complete*? It would certainly seem so. Yet Hegel has told us that in his system, philosophy arrives at its proper conclusion, and no other result can be more final than that. This poses an issue that continues to reverberate through philosophy, namely, whether a form of understanding that focuses on seeing the world in terms of becoming and change, that comprehends phenomena as parts of a restless, ongoing process, could ever consistently claim to be complete. I shall postpone further discussion of this issue until the final chapter and urge that in the meantime we join in admiration of the audacity and ambition of Hegel's philosophical quest. For range and depth he cannot be surpassed, and as his cleverest opponents have found out, you cannot go around him but must instead work your way through him in order to get beyond. There are very few other thinkers of whom this may be said, and of none is it truer than it is of Hegel.

NOTES

1. G. W. F. Hegel, *Hegel's Logic*, pt. 1 of the *Encyclopaedia of the Philosophical Sciences* (1830), trans. William Wallace, 3rd ed. (Oxford: Clarendon Press, 1975), sec. 1, p. 3. There are two complete English translations of this work in print (see also note 5). As with all quotations from Hegel that appear in this book, I shall select the translation that I believe best expresses both the letter and the spirit of his thought in the given instance. Consequently, alternation among available translations is intended to serve the dual purposes of clarity and faithfulness to the original. In his translation, Wallace describes the *Encyclopedia* as "the only complete, matured, and authentic statement of Hegel's philosophical system" ("Bibliographical Notice," p. xxxi).

2. Friedrich Nietzsche, *Daybreak: Thoughts on the Prejudices of Morality*, ed. Maudemarie Clark and Brian Leiter, trans. R. J. Hollingdale (Cambridge: Cambridge University Press, 1997), sec. 547, p. 220.

3. Hegel, *Hegel's Logic*, sec. 13, p. 19.

4. To the best of my knowledge, this expression was originated by Janice Moulton. See her essay "A Paradigm of Philosophy: The Adversary Method," in *Discovering Reality: Feminist Perspectives on Epistemology, Metaphysics, Methodology,*

and Philosophy of Science, ed. Sandra Harding and Merill B. Hintikka (Dordrecht: D. Reidel, 1983), pp. 149–64.

5. G. W. F. Hegel, *The Encyclopaedia Logic (Encyclopaedia of the Philosophical Sciences, Part I)*, trans. T. F. Geraets, W. A. Suchting, and H. S. Harris (Indianapolis: Hackett, 1991), sec. 2, p. 25.

6. Ibid.

7. Hegel, *Hegel's Logic*, sec. 60, pp. 91–92.

8. G. W. F. Hegel, *The Phenomenology of Spirit*, trans. A. V. Miller (Oxford: Clarendon Press, 1977), sec. 80, p. 51.

9. Richard Lovelace, "To Althea, from Prison" (1649), stanza 4.

10. Hegel, *Hegel's Logic*, sec. 60, p. 92 (emphasis in original).

11. Ibid., sec. 23, p. 35 (emphasis in original).

12. See Thomas Nagel, *The View from Nowhere* (New York: Oxford University Press, 1986).

13. G. W. F. Hegel, *Gesammelte Werke*, ed. Reinisch-Westfälische Akademie der Wissenschaften in association with the Deutsche Forschungsgemeinschaft (Hamburg: Felix Meiner, 1968 and ongoing).

14. Hegel interestingly observes that language, in its most rudimentary usage (that is, when it seeks to describe the contents of immediate experience), "possesses the divine nature of directly subverting, metamorphosing, and thus hindering the verbal expression of, meaning" because it expresses the universal, never really the particular *as* particular. See *Hegel's "Phenomenology of Spirit": Selections*, trans. Howard P. Kainz (University Park: Pennsylvania State University Press, 1994), sec. 110, p. 42. Only more refined, philosophical language can express the highest truth in a way that is adequate to the concepts it presents.

15. Hegel, *Hegel's Logic*, sec. 14, p. 19.

16. See, for example, Thomas S. Kuhn's *The Structure of Scientific Revolutions*, 2nd ed. (Chicago: University of Chicago Press, 1970), another highly influential text, for a classic example.

17. G. W. F. Hegel, *Lectures on the History of Philosophy*, trans. E. S. Haldane (London: Routledge and Kegan Paul; New York: Humanities Press, 1963), vol. 1, p. 37.

18. G. W. F. Hegel, introduction to *Lectures on the History of Philosophy*, trans. Quentin Lauer, in *Hegel's Idea of Philosophy*, by Lauer (New York: Fordham University Press, 1971), p. 83.

19. Ibid., p. 89 (emphasis in original). A parallel with the Australian Aborigines' "Dreamtime" is striking, since it too is a story held to be both past and actively present at the same time.

20. Hegel, *Hegel's Logic*, sec. 15, p. 20. Knowledge of this kind Hegel considers "infinite," that is, self-complete and free from external limitations.

21. This drawing provides only a very general representation of the way in which one might interrelate the branches of philosophy. It does not purport to

include *all* divisions of philosophy—according to Hegel's or to anyone else's schema; nor does it necessarily indicate the precise ways in which Hegel thought the areas of philosophical inquiry give rise to one another in the course of thought's advance.

22. Hegel, *Hegel's Logic*, sec. 17, pp. 22–23.

23. Søren Kierkegaard, *Concluding Unscientific Postscript to "Philosophical Fragments,"* trans. Howard V. Hong and Edna H. Hong (Princeton, NJ: Princeton University Press, 1992), vol. 1, p. 112.

24. Ernest LePore, "Semantic Holism," in *The Cambridge Dictionary of Philosophy*, ed. Robert Audi, 2nd ed. (Cambridge: Cambridge University Press, 1999), p. 829.

25. See, for example, Tom Rockmore, *Hegel's Circular Epistemology* (Bloomington: Indiana University Press, 1986), and Howard P. Kainz, *G. W. F. Hegel: The Philosophical System* (New York: Twayne; London: Prentice Hall International, 1996), chap. 1, sec. V, and chap. 3.

26. Arthur Schopenhauer, notwithstanding his constant pose as Hegel's nemesis, provides a very clear and helpful statement of the idealist position that is generally applicable: "the *subjective, our own consciousness* . . . [,] alone is and remains that which is immediate; everything else, be it what it may, is first mediated and conditioned by consciousness, and therefore dependent on it." See Schopenhauer, *The World as Will and Representation*, trans. E. F. J. Payne (New York: Dover, 1966), vol. 2, suppl. chap. 1, p. 4. (emphasis in original).

27. Hegel, *Hegel's Logic*, sec. 11, p. 15.

28. Hegel, *Encyclopaedia Logic*, sec. 12, p. 36.

29. Hegel, *Hegel's Logic*, sec. 12, p. 18 (emphasis in original).

2

DIALECTIC

BACKGROUND

In order to gain an accurate picture of Hegel's thought, nothing is more important than a good grasp of what he means by "dialectic." Anyone who has read a little ancient Greek philosophy will know that Plato (427–347 BCE) first introduced this term in giving an account of the teachings of his mentor Socrates (469–399 BCE), for whom "dialectic" referred to a type of argumentation that proceeds by question and answer and seeks to refute an opponent's viewpoint by revealing its logical flaws. For Plato himself, however, dialectic came to represent a philosophical pathway to the highest truth—knowledge of the eternal essences of things (the Forms) and ultimately of the Form of the Good. Hegel acknowledges that he did not invent dialectic and explains that his own "loftier dialectic of the concept" veers off in a quite distinct direction from the "negative mode which frequently appears even in Plato."[1]

Hegel sees the world as characterized most fundamentally by change, becoming, and opposition. All entities exist in a state of unsettled transition. The passage of time and the forces at work in nature give each thing only a limited period of duration. In addition, everything that exists is driven by conflicting tendencies, whether we speak of evolutionary competition among species, action and reaction in the nat-

.

ural world (e.g., force and counterforce, matter and antimatter), or antagonistic elements in the human sphere (e.g., war and peace, reason and feeling, dominance and submission, in-group and out-group). Hegel's philosophy, above all else, presents a tale of unity amid diversity, in which he attempts to fit the unstable, discordant, and ever-changing elements of thought and experience into a rational pattern of understanding. To this end, he resurrected, or, more precisely, reinvented, dialectic.

THE MEANINGS OF "DIALECTIC"

Dialectic, for Hegel, signifies five things: (1) the need to apprehend the world and everything in it as fluid, or as in the process of becoming; (2) a fruitful way of highlighting oppositional relationships; (3) a way of thinking through (and thereby absorbing mentally) opposing conceptions, with the aim of moving beyond them to a more "rational" and "higher" (more complete or more comprehensive) result; (4) the cumulative and self-transformative character of truth and knowledge; and, most intriguingly, (5) a force in the world that pervades and subverts all things and processes, leading them to their eventual ruin and annihilation, but also beyond this to a new, creative result. Let us consider these in turn.

(1) *Becoming*. The nineteenth century is viewed intellectually as, among other things, the era in which philosophers turned from an Aristotelian fixation on being to a concern with becoming. Instead of a picture of the world, or of reality, that focuses on the permanent, underlying nature of things (substances and essences), the changeable, restless, open-ended world of lived experience and fluid forms began to stimulate diverse thinkers. From Hegel to the early existentialists Kierkegaard and Nietzsche, to evolutionary theorists Jean-Baptiste de Lamarck and Charles Darwin, to process philosophers Henri Bergson and Alfred North Whitehead, this new preoccupation rapidly took hold. Hegel, as we shall see later on, sought a grasp of essences in addition to the changeable, but for him, these were to be found embedded in, and expressed by, the things of experience and not separable from them.

Hegel was arguably the most significant philosopher of becoming since ancient times. Whatever is, he asserted, is on its way to being something and, by the same token, is on its way to perishing. We may also say that what is beginning to be is moving from nonexistence to existence—as such, in a certain sense, or in certain respects. Furthermore, the essence of anything, its "what-ness" or "what-it-is-ness," is not simply given all at once; it develops and reveals itself as it emerges. A picture of reality, to be accurate therefore, must reflect the fact that existing things are constantly in transition. As Jean-Luc Nancy states, in explicating Hegel, "Everything is in the absolute restlessness of becoming. But becoming is not a process that leads to another thing, because it is the condition of every thing."[2] The "restlessness" of which Nancy speaks is the medium of becoming in which everything is immersed. Anything that exists, and any thought that we think about it, is equally affected (we might say "infected" or "afflicted") by becoming. The river of time flows ever onward, and there is no still backwater into which it is deflected, no calm sea into which it empties.

(2) *Opposing.* To ease our way into the type of thinking Hegel wants to press upon our attention, the following piece of popular culture trivia may be helpful. "Archie Andrews," a fictional comic book star known to most North Americans, first appeared on the scene in 1941. Archie was born a teenager and has remained a romantic, boisterous, sports-loving, and mischievous high school student, frozen in time, for more than sixty years. His life is always different, but always the same. It's as though Archie were continually undergoing the process Albert Einstein proposed as a mere thought-experiment—as if he were the one who travels the universe faster than the speed of light and scarcely ages at all, while the rest of us, left behind on earth, age mightily. Of course, all this is impossible, and we know it. Yet we like to pretend otherwise.[3]

Much of our entertainment is of just this kind: We make it possible only because we engage in a "willing suspension of disbelief." Movies, stage productions, novels, magic shows, theme parks, computer games, and virtual reality environments all share this feature in common. It is nicely captured by Jean-Paul Sartre in the following example:

On the stage of the music hall, Franconay is doing some impersonations.

> I recognize the person she is imitating; it is Maurice Chevalier. I appraise the imitation: "That really is Maurice Chevalier," or "It doesn't come off."
>
> What is going on in my consciousness? . . .
>
> How is Maurice Chevalier to be discovered in these plump painted cheeks, this dark hair, this female body, these female clothes? . . .

> [I]n the last analysis, only a definite act of will can keep con-
> sciousness from sliding from the level of the image to that of percep-
> tion. Even so, this sliding usually occurs at one moment or another. It
> often happens that the synthesis is not completely carried out: the face
> and body of the impersonator do not lose all of their individuality;
> but the expressive something "Maurice Chevalier" nevertheless
> appears on this face, on this female body. A hybrid state develops,
> which is neither entirely perceptive nor entirely imaginative. . . . This
> unstable and transitory state is obviously what is most entertaining for
> the spectator in an impersonation.[4]

As Sartre observes, Franconay both *is* and *is not* Maurice Chevalier, and
the entertainment we are provided by this spectacle derives from the
duplicity of consciousness on this score, plus its ability to fluctuate
comfortably between believing and not-believing, seeing and not-
seeing, perceiving and imagining.

In *The Invisible Man*, Ralph Ellison refers to "the novel's capacity for
telling the truth while actually telling a 'lie.'"[5] This kind of observation
about the paradoxical nature of fictional works not only underscores
Hegel's observations concerning the presence of "contradiction"
throughout everyday life and experience but also highlights a problem
that has supplied raw material for many philosophical minds. The
problem is the following: How can an admittedly *false* fictional world
serve as a vehicle for making purportedly *true* statements about ourselves and the real world we inhabit? We cannot investigate this interesting question here, but it is worth noting that Ellison, by placing the
word "lie" within quotation marks, indicates that what seems to be a lie
really is not; there is (or, at any rate, evidently must be) a way to resolve
the apparent contradiction, though we are not told what that way might
be or how it works. Hegel, as we shall see, does try to tell us just that.

One further example, also selected from a fictional work, will help
illustrate the prevalence of contradiction in experience, when we consider it in the broadest sense.

> It was the best of times, it was the worst of times, it was the age of
> wisdom, it was the age of foolishness, it was the epoch of belief, it was
> the epoch of incredulity, it was the season of Light, it was the season
> of Darkness, it was the spring of hope, it was the winter of despair, we
> had everything before us, we had nothing before us, we were all going
> direct to Heaven, we were all going direct the other way.

For many readers, this famous opening sentence of Charles Dickens's *A Tale of Two Cities* not only sounds familiar but also rings true. It conveys an insight that applies to our own time—or to any time—and the author achieves a powerful impact completely by means of the device of making assertions and simultaneously negating and thereby revoking them.

Disagreement and conflict are commonplace features of interpersonal dealings as well as of our own conscious states. Thus, we speak often of "being at cross-purposes," "clashes of opinion," "ideological struggles," and so on, and at the personal level, of "conflicting emotions," "being of two minds about something," "self-criticism," "self-denial," "self-deception," and so forth. We use sarcasm, irony, and metaphor throughout our speech, saying and not saying at one and the same time, playing on self-canceling meanings and assumed but hidden levels of meaning. As Portuguese novelist José Saramago remarks, "The human spirit, though, how often do we need to say it, is the favourite home of contradictions, indeed they do not seem to prosper or even find viable living conditions outside it."[6] (Hegel would agree with the first part of this statement, even if not the second.) Sigmund Freud (1856–1939) also held a powerful Hegelian view of the self. According to one physician, who kept copious notes on his psychoanalytic sessions with the master, "Freud presented a kind of dialectical picture of personality, as composed of many conflicting tendencies, both good and bad, and scorned the simpler formulas of common parlance, or of the fashionable science of his time."[7]

None of us are really strangers to the dialectical in experience or to the fact that interpersonal and intrapsychic conflicts frequently remain unresolved. Hegel possessed sophisticated knowledge of these phenomena that he uses to enrich our understanding of them. However, he held a much deeper view of dialectical interactions and of the factors involved in their resolution or nonresolution, as I shall now explain.

Oppositional relationships of any kind, in the physical world or in the realm of ideas, are not taken at face value by Hegel. Rather, he sees beyond confrontation and contention to an equally important factor of dependency and complementarity, and it is this that opens the way to their possible resolution. To take some simple examples, black and white, good and bad, night and day, finite and infinite, life and death, one and many: these are all opposed pairs, but in each case the meaning of one term involves or "points to" the meaning of its opposite. What is designated by each concept would be indistinguishable as what it is without at least implicit reference to its opposite. For instance, if we lived in everlasting daylight, we would not identify it as anything other than the normal state of affairs, as there'd be nothing with which to contrast it. There might not even be a word for "day" in our language. In general, only features of experience or ideas that have such possibilities of contrast built into them are singled out by us for special attention and deemed important enough to be captured by language. A Yiddish proverb nicely crystalizes the point: "When one always drinks vinegar, he doesn't know that anything sweeter exists." ("*Az men trinkt ale mol esik, veyst men nit az es iz do a zisere zakh.*")[8] One further example will prove enlightening as well. It has often been noted that many indigenous peoples of the world refer to themselves in their own languages simply as "The People" because traditionally they had no contact with human strangers of diverse origins and cultures.[9] There was thus no need for their languages to reflect their own identities with any more precision than this, much less in a vocabulary of difference.

But Hegel has considerably more in mind. He also holds that everything is constituted as much by what it expresses positively as by what it suppresses or excludes negatively.[10] This is both an ontological claim (about the way things *are*) and an epistemological assertion (about how we *know* about things). A red object, for instance, is what it is by virtue of possessing a certain property, redness, but it is equally true of it (and equally important to note) that it *is* red by *not-being* yellow, green, blue, and so forth. To be red is to "banish" or "repel" other possible colors. The latter, "negative," counterpart of our knowledge is usually either ignored or we are oblivious to it, but it functions just as crucially in our experience and cognition and is just as formative of them as its "positive" aspect. One could state this point as follows: All attribution or predication (i.e., every form of description) is at the same time an act of privation, of taking away or exclusion. To ascribe a property to something can be thought of as prohibiting attachment to it of other attributes of an incompatible or even a similar sort. "X is red" entails "X is not violet" (the most extreme contrasting wavelength), but it also entails "X is not yellow, green, blue, and so forth," as we have seen. On the other hand, "P is kind" excludes "P is cruel" (its opposite), but not necessarily "P has very good social skills," "P is thrifty," "P is lazy," "P is sexually abusive of children," and other different personality and behavioral traits commonly accepted as being able to coexist with kindness. We shall examine in greater detail in the next chapter just how

Hegel uses this feature of the world and of language to propel his philosophical investigations. For the moment, however, it is important to
take note of his claim that each entity is a tension of conflicting elements; each exists in a juxtaposition of relatedness and unrelatedness
vis-à-vis others; metaphorically speaking, each "contains" its opposite
within itself. As the poet Percy Bysshe Shelley elegantly stated:

> Nothing in the world is single;
> All things by a law divine
> In one another's being mingle—[11]

(3) *Thinking*. It is regularly (but erroneously) supposed that wher-
ever Hegel discerned opposing tendencies he posited a "thesis" and an
"antithesis," which yield ground eventually to an all-embracing "synthesis." This is an unfortunate caricature, as it makes his rich and complex way of thinking into a merely mechanical recipe to be rigidly
imposed upon our sundry observations. That this stereotype has come
to be almost indelibly associated with Hegel is ironic, especially since he
himself denounced such recipes as "lifeless schemas" and as examples of
"monotonous formalism."[12] It would therefore be more faithful to his
intent to appreciate how rival viewpoints, opposing forces, and sociocultural conflicts come to be resolved or reexpressed in a new guise.

Electricity and magnetism can serve as elementary examples. Each
of these phenomena exhibits positive and negative polarities. These do
not normally abrogate one another, however, but jointly create a force
that performs work and has effects we can put to use. Electricity and
magnetism are therefore "dialectical" in nature. But so similarly are
many things in the domain of human events and ideas. In a labor
versus management confrontation where arbitration takes place, for
instance, the ideal goal is to find a basis for agreement that represents a
"win-win" solution. Both sides get something they were after while
making concessions, and no one loses outright. (By contrast a "zero-
sum" solution has one side winning and the other losing, in like pro-
portions.) And what happens to the original opposition? A faithful
Hegelian would say that it doesn't disappear; rather, it becomes transformed by, and assimilated into, the solution, where it remains present
as an active ingredient. Like the Phoenix rising from the ashes, like pine
seeds whose germination starts only with a forest fire, the new is always
an outgrowth of the old, nourished by the latter's decomposition.

A time-worn motto that surfaces in many fields (e.g., sociology, ecology, gestalt psychology, and philosophy) is that "the whole is greater than the sum of its parts." Hegel certainly subscribes to this position for two main reasons: (a) the parts that make up a whole each have a history of how they came to be connected, and they carry this history with them, so that understanding this background is essential to understanding the whole and the parts' place in it, and (b) the whole always represents a new "emergence" out of the parts, in other words, a transformation of them into a new product or form of coexisting elements. In one of his most memorable images, these ideas are beautifully conveyed:

> The bud disappears in the bursting-forth of the blossom, and one might say that the former is refuted by the latter; similarly, when the fruit appears, the blossom is shown up in its turn as a false manifestation of the plant, and the fruit now emerges as the truth of it instead. These forms are not just distinguished from one another, they also supplant one another as mutually incompatible. Yet at the same time their fluid nature makes them moments of an organic unity in which they not only do not conflict, but in which each is as necessary as the other; and this mutual necessity alone constitutes the life of the whole.[13]

The plant's blossoming is incompatible with its budding, and its fructification, likewise, with its blossoming; in each case the former state comes forth only by virtue of the "negation" of its predecessor. However, to view a unitary development in this manner is to dissect and fragment what belongs essentially together. The plant has a life (a history), and this life courses through time. In a similar vein, when one views philosophical systems of the past as competitors standing in such a relationship to one another that they are mutually antagonistic, reciprocally "refuting," and nothing more, one fails to discern the organic growth of knowledge that comprises them all. Consequently, the "truth" of which Hegel speaks is what emerges at each stage when previous developments are superseded, both phases being viewed as integral parts of a single process.

What, precisely, is meant by "emergence" here? Many philosophers (but by no means all) contend that this is a frequently observed characteristic of change. Water molecules, as we know, are made up of two parts hydrogen and one part oxygen. Now, the argument goes that if we knew in advance all the properties of hydrogen and oxygen taken separately—except for their tendency to combine with each other to form water—we would be unable to predict that when reacting together in a certain way, they would produce a liquid substance that is odorless, tasteless, colorless, a universal solvent, expands when frozen, supports life, and so forth. What happens here (when H_2O is created) is that *quantitative* change leads to *qualitative* change, and emergent properties are the result. The elements H and O are still present, but are transformed by a chemical reaction into something new, with unforeseen, even unforeseeable, characteristics and capacities. Not only this; the hydrogen and oxygen each lose their stand-alone properties in the product, water—or perhaps we should say these become latent, since they will reassert themselves if the reaction is reversed. Similar arguments have been presented on behalf of life as an emergent product of matter at a certain level of complex organization and of society as an emergent product of the interactions among the individuals that make it up. (Hegel, in fact, defends this view of society, as we shall observe in chapter 6.) In like manner, it could be claimed, all significant change involves an analogous aspect of emergence (often called "synergy").

It is time to become acquainted with another key ingredient of Hegel's reflections on dialectic. This is the multifaceted meaning of the word *aufheben*, which is the term he uses to refer to the result of a dialectical process, as will be explained presently. Hegel's texts often employ the German words *aufheben* (a verb) and *Aufhebung* (the related noun). It is unfortunate that these are normally translated as "to sublate" and "sublation," respectively, because these English words have little or no meaning to the modern reader. Sometimes the German terms are rendered as "to sublimate" and "sublimation," respectively, which may convey more sense, but their usefulness is compromised by the special usage to which Nietzsche and, later, Freud assigned them, namely, that of labeling the process by which we unconsciously channel instinctual impulses into alternative, socially more acceptable pathways (e.g., sexual energy into artistic endeavor or aggression into sports). Much better alternatives, in my opinion, though a bit more cumbersome, are the expressions "to dialectically supersede" and "dialectical supersession." Now that we have encountered the idea of emergence, speaking this way gains some intelligibility and begins to become instructive. When something is dialectically superseded, it is surpassed toward a new result in which the old state is implicit, but transformed.

Hegel likes to think in threes, so it will perhaps come as no surprise to the reader to learn that our philosopher detects a triple set of connotations attaching to the special terms he uses to characterize change in a dialectical fashion. *Aufheben* means, first of all, to destroy, cancel, annul, negate. Second, it means to preserve, maintain, keep. Third, it means to elevate, raise up, transform. Given all this, it is no wonder he chose to make this concept a centerpiece of his thought, for the word itself is dialectical, in that it contains opposing yet coexisting and interdependent elements of meaning. The main point here, however, is that when Hegel employs these words he tells us that we are witnessing a process whose original elements, aspects, or active agencies are in one sense canceled, in another sense preserved, but in an overall sense transfigured in such a way as to reappear, metamorphosed, in the result or within a later stage of the process. Returning to our water example, hydrogen and oxygen are "canceled" in that they are no longer capable of exhibiting their unique properties; they are "preserved" in that they participate together in a chemical reaction and are not lost; and they are "transformed" in that an emergent substance, water, is produced, which would not exist in their absence. The elements remain in a sort of quasi-resolved tension in the product, exercising their potency in and through it.

The examples discussed thus far illustrate a point that Hegel shares in common with certain forms of Eastern thought—that an entity is defined as much by what it *is not* as by what it *is*. We could also say, from the standpoint of the entity, that what is "other" both plays a vital role in defining it and at the same time acts as its limit (i.e., what-it-is-not—those properties that, if instantiated by it, would change its nature or character and make it into something different from what it is). In this sense what an entity is depends on what it is not; those features it possesses are contingent on the ones it lacks. In other words, it depends on what it is related to as its other for being what it is. The moral of the story is that *we never properly comprehend anything in its isolated particularity, but only in connection with other things and events.* It is not a big step from this claim to the view that all relationships are "internal," that is, that they make a difference to the things related or actively constitute them. A further incremental step takes us to the idea that all entities are interlinked or bound together in the web of being, and, likewise, the web of understanding.[14] Thought, in other words, reflects the way things are, deep within their own nature.

Some familiar associations may have arisen already in the reader's mind. One possibility is the Taoist concept of yang and yin. These are "the complementary principles through which the Tao is expressed."[15] The Tao, or way of the universe, is that which makes everything happen and manifests itself in both the yang modes of activity, day, rationality, speaking, the "masculine," and so on, and in the yin modes of receptivity, night, intuition, listening, the "feminine," and others. Yang and yin fit together to make a harmonious whole, and an ideal person or culture strives to incorporate both. Each limits but also sets off the other as its dependent opposite.

In this readily recognized symbol the interrelationship among opposites is portrayed very clearly. The dots of black and white embedded in each other's territory reinforce the insight that things "contain" their opposites within themselves.

Similar notions reappear in Buddhist and Zen thought, where we find that water is seen as capable of being by turns either strong and destructive or quiet and soothingly enveloping. We must take care to acknowledge and respect water for the contrasting

Yang and Yin.

sides of its nature. We can learn from it and gain an understanding of how to work with it and, by extension, with the conditions of life and with nature as a whole. A vase is both a solid, hard container yet equally an emptiness that receives whatever we wish to fill it with. While the outside is what we see and customarily identify as its "essence," without the emptiness or "nothingness" of its inside, it would not be a vase and would entirely lack its characteristic functionality. For a final illustration, consider these words of the contemporary Vietnamese Buddhist monk Thich Nhat Hanh: "Wealth is made of non-wealth elements, and poverty is made by non-poverty elements. It is exactly the same as with the sheet of paper [that is made of non-paper elements]. So we must be careful not to imprison ourselves in concepts. The truth is that everything contains everything else. We cannot just be, we can only inter-be. We are responsible for everything that happens around us."[16] Hanh says here that a subtle ecology links all things that exist, a mutual dependency that typically goes unnoticed and seldom receives conscious acknowledgment.

Things and events are determined by their opposites, which, as inseparable from them and yet distinct, both are and are not the same, both are
and are not identical with them. This attraction and repulsion nevertheless creates connection. Small wonder that there is considerable interest
in Hegel in China, India, and Japan.

The idea that opposites are interrelated and define one another, as
we have seen, conveys an insight that is truly cross-cultural. Consider
for a moment these remarks made by Banjo (Henry) Clarke, an Australian aboriginal elder, which provide yet another instance: "Everything in life has got to be in pairs of opposites that unite and make a
whole. . . . Nothing is really separate. Everything has to take into
account everything else. . . . Everything spiritual has its physical part,
and everything physical has its spiritual part."[17] For Clarke, this piece of
traditional wisdom expresses a way of life, a lived reality, not merely a
personal opinion or a philosophical theory. It is verified by everyday
experience, which is a fusion of perceptual and spiritual elements.
Hegel could not agree more.

(4) *Truthing*. While "truthing" is not a real word, or at best has collo-
quial meaning,[18] I am using it to indicate that for Hegel, truth is something that develops over time. It is the outcome of a process of reflection
in which we seek more adequate concepts for expressing what we know.
More precisely, it is the result of coming to know: Knowledge is an
achievement, a happening, not a fixed state. Consequently, truth, for
Hegel, is like a living organism because it grows into what it is to become.
And the coming-to-be of the truth (or of knowledge) is integral to the end
reached. Furthermore, and importantly, an evolution of concepts is necessary for truth to emerge fully. Thought progresses and modifies itself as
it explores its territory, and every step it takes helps yield the result. As
Stephen Priest remarks, "Truth is accumulative and gained by reflection
on the inadequacy of concepts in their use." Such inadequacy is remedied
by "their revision and enrichment in use."[19] Because thought revises itself
and sets its own standards of attainment, it is constantly opposing itself—
overcoming its own formulations—and is therefore dialectical in its very
nature. The truth, for Hegel, accordingly, is reached by this same means.
Since I will take up Hegel's concept of truth in detail in chapter 5, further
discussion of these interesting ideas will be postponed until then.

(5) *Perishing*. According to those who attended his lectures, Hegel
spoke of dialectic as a voracious agency that consumes everything in its
path. Here is an example of his rhetoric, reconstructed from their notes:

[Dialectic] is in general the principle of all motion, of all life, and of all activation in the actual world. . . . Everything around us can be regarded as an example of dialectic. For we know that, instead of being fixed and ultimate, everything finite is alterable and perishable, and this is nothing but the dialectic of the finite, through which the latter, being implicitly the other of itself, is driven beyond what it immediately is and overturns into its opposite. . . . We say that all things (i.e., everything finite as such) come to judgment, and in that saying we catch sight of the dialectic as the universal, irresistible might before which nothing can subsist, however firm and secure it may deem itself.[20]

Dialectic, this passage asserts, is a physical presence in the world, a force, or rather the Force of forces, the energizing originator of all change and development. But Hegel also tells us that dialectic is the "indwelling tendency" of every thing to turn into its opposite by becoming something different or by being transformed into a new state.[21] A piece of clay worked by the potter turns from a round ball into a flat plate. Is it the same entity or a different one? This is a classical philosophical puzzle concerning the nature and criteria of identity. Hegel wants to say that the clay's malleability turns it from one thing into another while it yet retains its fundamental identity as clay. Leave the clay alone, however, and it will dry out, crack, and eventually crumble into dust. The child grows into an adult. She is different in many ways; we might even say a different person. Yet she is the same because there is continuity of identity, though it is difficult to specify precisely in what this consists. The adult grows old and eventually dies. Here we have a more striking example of change where it is not merely new properties or traits that come on the scene and accumulate; instead, dissolution and destruction occur. Hegel's students report that he was fond of the image that "life as such bears the germ of death within itself, and the finite sublates itself because it contradicts itself inwardly."[22] In our age, with talk of "biological clocks" and genetically encoded triggering mechanisms in the human body, this formulation strikes one as not so far-fetched. More generally, he asserts, "That is what everything finite is: its own sublation."[23] In other words, everything embodies the principle of dialectical opposition within itself, which is a somewhat picturesque way of observing that both its attributes and its very composition are conditioned by relatedness, temporality, movement, mutability—and ultimate evanescence and self-demolition.

A VIOLATION OF THE LAWS OF LOGIC?

Having gained a reasonable inroad into what Hegel means by dialectic, we shall now consider one of the most persistent and potentially damaging criticisms his philosophy faces. This is that in praising and exalting the contradictory, Hegel violates the basic "laws of thought," and thus renders both language and reason self-stultifying and unusable. Specifically, it has been alleged that Hegel "denies the law of noncontradiction." What does this charge amount to? The law of noncontradiction (so-called) is an elementary, axiomatic principle of logic that states: "A sentence and its negation (i.e., its denial) cannot both be true; alternatively, nothing can be both P and not-P."[24] Thus, for example, the statements "This figure is a square" and "This figure is not a square" are contradictories: They cannot both be true *and* they cannot both be false; the case must be one way or the other. Each asserts what the other denies and denies what the other asserts; they posit exclusive alternatives. Something either is a square or it is not; you cannot have it both ways (or, for that matter, neither way). We have to choose in order to communicate meaningfully, for contradictory statements exhaust the field of possible discourse and when uttered together yield nonsense. Does Hegel try to have it both ways? Is he flirting with meaninglessness? First, we need to determine what he actually says.

As we saw above, Hegel contends that whatever is finite is radically self-contradictory. We might interpret this as simply his way of calling attention to the transitory nature of things, as already explained. But he has something more significant in mind, which is that by its very nature "thinking gets entangled in contradictions."[25] And again: "To see that thought in its very nature is dialectical, and that, as understanding, it must fall into contradiction—the negative of itself—will form one of the main lessons of logic."[26] That things change into their opposites, at least to the extent that they become what they were not a moment, a day, a year, a millennium, a geological era ago, is one of Hegel's central teachings. If the world is like this, then thought and language have to be capable of reflecting and capturing the fact, otherwise reality cannot be comprehended or communicated by us. Therefore, thought itself must be fluid in order to do justice to a world of constant flux and becoming, and so likewise must language be. Consequently, those statements that are made definitively at one time turn out to be less apposite or even completely inapplicable at another time. To place them side by side may yield a contradiction, but this is only apparent, as they were made (accurately), each with a different temporal frame of reference. "This is square" (uttered at time t_1) is not necessarily in conflict with "This is not square" (uttered at time t_2), since the shapes of things can and do undergo alteration.

Sometimes what appears to be a contradiction is the result of not specifying the respect in which statements are being asserted. "The table is white" and "The table is not white" look contradictory, but if suitable qualifiers are added, indicating that from different angles it looks to be first one, then the other, the initial ambivalence and mystery are resolved. Or if it is the case that the table is in part white and in part some other color, we can again rest at ease. Logic remains unviolated.

By now it should be evident that Hegel neither affirmed contradictory statements nor denied the law of contradiction; nor, I believe, was he in any way confused about his position on these matters. Perhaps a poet such as Walt Whitman can indulge himself differently, as when he declares:

Do I contradict myself?
Very well then I contradict myself,
(I am large, I contain multitudes.)[27]

But for a philosopher so taken up with the task of painstakingly detailing a rational worldview as Hegel, this attitude would never do. It is the vocation of thought to rise above contradictions, to heal the internal rifts that it causes. We do not stop when contradictions appear that threaten to defeat thought; we persist and find a way to move beyond them. Thought "dissolves" the otherness of the other and assimilates it into a larger framework of intelligibility. Thus, thought does not accept internal disagreement of ideas as a final result or resting point.[28] When thought limits itself to "understanding," the mode we employ most characteristically in everyday life, this is when we get into trouble. Taking the terms in their technical Hegelian sense, it is *understanding* (*Verstand*), as opposed to *reason* (*Vernunft*), that rigidly juxtaposes statements and descriptive categories of things. This tendency of understanding to separate and draw fixed distinctions is useful—even necessary—in our ordinary dealings with the world. But when we try to think more creatively (as a poet or a speculative philosopher does), we operate within a more inclusive or relational array of ideas and images (for example, using metaphors or nonstandard theoretical constructs), and this leads us to contradictions. *Reason*, on the other hand, signifies the kind of thinking that helps us move beyond such logical obstacles.[29] For reason helps us find patterns within which opposing concepts can be fit and made to work together. Using reason signifies the act of transforming contradictions, by means of a higher effort of cognition, into novel forms of comprehension, wherein opposites are each given their due.

Hegel was acutely aware that the nature of the world and of lived experience is contradictory, as the many examples I have given serve to indicate. This does not mean he spoke with a forked tongue or wrote books full of self-eliminating, nonsensical sentences. He was as far from adopting the pose of an inscrutable guru as one can imagine. Indeed, it was his very *respect* for the law of noncontradiction that led him to seek ways to overcome the seemingly contradictory formulations in which he believed thought defiantly entangles itself when it inadequately grasps its own subject matter. This is the "lesson of logic" that Hegel urges us to learn with his guidance.

CAVEATS

Two final points remain to be made. The first is that we should not suppose that whenever the evolution of knowledge or belief is viewed dialectically, this automatically entails that an irreversible shift from some position to its opposite is taking place. This is the error in attributing a thesis-antithesis-synthesis structure to Hegel's method of reasoning. While it is true that a dialectical process involves opposing moments, an initial position, now strengthened by critical scrutiny, may be the emergent result. For example, when one begins to study philosophy, one may have a firm faith in the veracity of sense-perception or perhaps in the existence of God. Coming into contact with skeptical arguments concerning either, this faith is likely to be shaken, at least initially, if not eroded entirely. However, as often happens, after further study and deeper self-questioning, one again finds reason to believe, but now with full recognition of the philosophical problems generated by such commitments, and this calls forth, in turn, certain ways of dealing with the objections these problems have produced. The dialectical result, then, is a more sophisticated or enriched position incorporating the issues that have been reviewed and surmounted. John Stuart

Mill (aided by his wife, Harriet Taylor Mill) made the same point in the context of a famous and spirited defense of unlimited free speech in the essay *On Liberty*. The argument there is that unrestricted debate strengthens democracy because if beliefs are allowed to go unchallenged, they lose vitality and stagnate. On the other hand, beliefs that are regularly challenged have a much improved chance of being "better" or "truer" (hardier and more resilient) than the alternatives. Interestingly, the following quite Hegelian statement accompanies Mill's exposition: "Every opinion which embodies somewhat of the portion of truth which the common opinion omits, ought to be considered precious, with whatever amount of error and confusion that truth may be blended."[30] As we shall see in chapter 5, for Hegel truth and falsity are indeed intertwined and necessary complementaries.

Second, Hegel did not regard his investigation of the dialectical nature of thought as the invention of a new method for doing philosophy so much as an act of unearthing and featuring the actual, natural dynamic of self-conscious reasoning. Philosophers had hitherto hinted at this insight in various ways but had never before articulated or applied it to the solution of perennial problems. Nor is dialectic merely a curious structural feature of detached, intellectual theorizing. Rather, it is, as we have seen, the very essence of thought itself, no matter what it is trained upon.

NOTES

1. G. W. F. Hegel, *Elements of the Philosophy of Right*, ed. Allen W. Wood, trans. H. B. Nisbet (Cambridge: Cambridge University Press, 1991), sec. 31, p. 60.

2. Jean-Luc Nancy, *Hegel: The Restlessness of the Negative*, trans. Jason Smith and Steven Miller (Minneapolis: University of Minnesota Press, 2002), p. 12.

3. For a fascinating discussion of time and other dimensions of the comic book world, see Umberto Eco, "The Myth of Superman," in his *The Role of the Reader: Explorations in the Semiotics of Texts*, trans. Natalie Chilton (Bloomington: Indiana University Press, 1979).

4. Jean-Paul Sartre, *The Psychology of the Imagination*, trans. Bernard Frechtman (rev. Robert Denoon Cumming), excerpted in *The Philosophy of Jean-Paul Sartre*, ed. R. D. Cumming (New York: Modern Library, 1966), pp. 81, 84, 86.

5. Ralph Ellison, *The Invisible Man* (New York: Vintage Books, 1989), p. xxii.

6. José Saramago, *All the Names*, trans. Margaret Jull Costa (San Diego: Harcourt, 2001), p. 228.

7. Joseph Wortis, *Fragments of an Analysis with Freud* (New York: Simon and Schuster, 1954), p. 189.

8. Benjamin Blech, *The Complete Idiot's Guide to Learning Yiddish* (Indianapolis: Alpha Books, Macmillan USA, 2000), p. 248.

9. Two examples: the Inuit (see http://collections.ic.gc.ca/arctic/inuit/people.htm) and the Navajo (see www.nps.gov/nava/nav.htm).

10. See, for example, G. W. F. Hegel, *Hegel's Logic*, pt. 1 of *Encyclopaedia of the Philosophical Sciences*, trans. William Wallace, 3rd ed. (Oxford: Clarendon Press, 1975), secs. 117–20, pp. 169–75 (*The Encyclopaedia Logic*, trans. T. F. Geraets, W. A. Suchting, and H. S. Harris [Indianapolis: Hackett, 1991], pp. 182–88).

11. Percy Bysshe Shelley, "Love's Philosophy" (1819).

12. G. W. F. Hegel, preface to *The Phenomenology of Spirit*, trans. A. V. Miller (Oxford: Clarendon Press, 1977), secs. 50, 51, pp. 29, 30.

13. Ibid., sec. 2, p. 2.

14. Comparisons with the kinds of interconnection and interdependence found in ecology and in Buddhist philosophy, I suggest, are irresistible.

15. Helen Buss Mitchell, *Roots of Wisdom*, 4th ed. (Belmont, CA: Wadsworth Thomson Learning, 2005), p. 73.

16. Thich Nhat Hanh, *Peace Is Every Step: The Path of Mindfulness in Everyday Life* (New York: Bantam, 1991), p. 98.

17. Banjo Clarke (as told to Camilla Chance), *Wisdom Man* (Camberwell, Australia: Viking/Penguin, 2003), p. 218.

18. The singer Nancy Sinatra once recorded a popular song called "These Boots Are Made for Walkin'," written by Lee Hazlewood, which contains the line: "You keep lyin' when you shoulda been truthin'."

19. Stephen Priest, introduction to *Hegel's Critique of Kant*, ed. Stephen Priest (Oxford: Clarendon Press, 1987), p. 19.

20. Hegel, *Encyclopaedia Logic*, sec. 81, pp. 128–29, 130.

21. Hegel, *Hegel's Logic*, sec. 81, p. 116.

22. Hegel, *Encyclopaedia Logic*, sec. 81, p. 129. Cf. sec. 92, p. 149. Hegelian thoughts like this were the inspiration for the well-known Marxist doctrine of the "internal contradictions of capitalism" that will someday lead to the collapse of this system and what Friedrich Engels called the "withering away of the state."

23. Ibid., sec. 81, p. 128.

24. Robert M. Martin, *The Philosopher's Dictionary*, 3rd ed. (Peterborough, Canada: Broadview Press, 2003), p. 177.

25. Hegel, *Encyclopaedia Logic*, sec. 11, p. 35.

26. Hegel, *Hegel's Logic*, sec. 11, p. 15.

27. Walt Whitman, *Song of Myself* (1855; final rev. 1881), sec. 51.

28. It is here that Hegel parts company with some varieties of Eastern thought, inasmuch as he insists that reason can resolve "contradictions," whereas Zen, for example, demurs, requiring of us that we develop non-rational avenues to insight and accept the nonresolution of contradictions.

29. Also referred to by Hegel as "speculative thinking" or "the thinking that comprehends." See the translation of the preface to *Phenomenology of Spirit*, in *Hegel: Texts and Commentary*, trans. Walter Kaufmann (Notre Dame, IN: University of Notre Dame Press, 1977), sec. IV.1, pp. 88–101. See also Hegel, *Phenomenology of Spirit*, trans. Miller, secs. 58–66, pp. 35–41.

30. John Stuart Mill, *On Liberty* in *Utilitarianism, Liberty, and Representative Government* (New York: E. P. Dutton; London: J. M. Dent and Sons, 1951), chap. 2, p. 141.

3

VISION, METHOD, AND SYSTEM

ORIGINS OF METAPHYSICAL THINKING

The quest for a general theory of reality—one that accounts for the nature of the world and human beings' place in the scheme of things—is as old as intelligence itself. Aristotle (384–322 BCE) was the first Western philosopher to state that metaphysics is a natural disposition, that is, an activity humans cannot help pursuing, and one that has intrinsic value: "All men by nature desire to know. . . . [I]t is owing to their wonder that men both now begin and at first began to philosophize. . . . Evidently then we do not seek [metaphysical knowledge] for the sake of any other advantage. . . . [but only] for its own sake."[1] Most of our lives are lived in the mode of taking things more or less for granted, and our normal encounters with the world are nonmomentous, routine, and unproblematic. Yet the time arrives for assessment and self-questioning, when we strive to put it all together and make sense of the world. This is the kind of pivotal point about which Aristotle spoke.

A little over a century ago, writing from within a very different cultural temperament, philosopher F. H. Bradley (1846–1924) modified this age-old view about our need for speculative thinking by formulating the following paradox: "Metaphysics is the finding of bad reasons for what we believe upon instinct, but to find these reasons is no less an instinct."[2] As Bradley would have it, the metaphysical pursuit is indeed unavoidable and second nature for humans, but the trouble is, he thinks, what we discover translates very poorly into concepts and words.

Where metaphysics comes from—or, alternatively, where philosophers get their ideas about what reality must ultimately be like—has always been a puzzle to those who step back from this enterprise in order to question it critically. Hegel would have agreed with both Aristotle and Bradley about the instinctual urgency of metaphysical rumination. But he would have disagreed emphatically with the latter that our speculative accounts are framed in terms of bad reasons. So where did Hegel get *his* deeper insights from, and how did he justify them? The explanatory support Hegel provides for his metaphysical outlook will occupy a great deal of our attention later on. Concerning the *source* of his insights, history does not tell us the answer to our question, but I will venture to state, as a general theory about metaphysics, that for many of its great, original practitioners, such as Plato, Baruch Spinoza, Arthur Schopenhauer, Hegel, Henri Bergson, Martin Heidegger, and Alfred North Whitehead in the West, a fundamental vision was at the root of their inspiration. This is not necessarily the result of an epiphany, though it might be. Instead, let us call it "intuition," "mystical awareness," "religious experience," or "an expanded form of consciousness." Whatever expression we choose, the central notion is still the same, namely, that metaphysics is the attempt to render communicable some discernment about the nature of things, revealed in one or more flashes of privileged experience.

There are those who regard such a grasp of the truth as ineffable; for Hegel, however, this was wrong. He insists, controversially, that the deepest insights into the nature of things can be intelligibly communicated. Indeed, it was his credo that anything worthy of being referred to as knowledge of reality as a whole must be capable of translation into thought and language. As he colorfully pronounced, "Reason refuses to allow feeling to warm itself by its own private hearth."[3] Hegel also believed that new ideas, conceptions, and theories that seem to appear in consciousness as if from nowhere are actually the products of a slower process of germination and gestation. They may be launched in a special creative moment, but to be of any lasting significance, they require refinement and reexpression in the medium of rational cognition and through meaningful discourse.

While I have suggested that Hegel derived his inspiration from a fundamental vision of reality, it is clear that his motivation was of quite a different kind from that of mystics and poets. Repeatedly, he tells us things like the following: that "the expression 'visionary dreaming' sums up, once and for all, what philosophy means to those who are ignorant of it" and that there is no "royal road" to metaphysical understanding.[4] Philosophy is a serious activity for dedicated people, aiming at clarity, organized knowing, and publicly shared results. Perhaps, then, Hegel would reject my characterization of his thought as springing from a primal vision? I do not think so, and to see why, we need to distinguish between what I call a vision and what Hegel labels as "visionary dreaming." The former is a spark or catalyst that ignites a reasoning process; the latter is idle musing, unstructured guesswork or the product of aesthetic emotion—the kind of thing that, then as now, gives philosophy a bad name and associates it with undisciplined fantasizing. More than once, he rails against "those who begin [philosophizing], like a shot from a pistol, from their inner revelation, from faith, intellectual intuition, etc., and who would be exempt from *method* and logic."[5] Hegel was very sensitive to uninformed perspectives on what philosophy is all about, but as well, he denounced Romantic thinkers and those under their influence who believe it is nothing more than drifting along in a state of reverie, letting feelings hold sway. Both critiques are embedded in this passage, where he complains:

> Philosophic science is often treated with contempt by those who imagine and say—although they have not made any effort to come to grips with it—that they already understand what philosophy is all about quite spontaneously, and that they are able to do philosophy and to judge it just by holding on to what they have learnt at a very ordinary level, in particular from their religious feelings. In the case of the other sciences, we admit that one has to have studied them in order to know about them, and that one is only entitled to judge them in virtue of a studied acquaintance. We admit that in order to make a shoe, one has to have learnt and practiced how to do it, even though every one of us has the required measure in his own feet, and we all have hands with a natural aptitude for the trade in question. It is only for doing philosophy that study, learning, and effort of this kind is supposedly not needed.[6]

However accurate this appraisal may be today, and however fair the characterization of his opponents, Hegel has a point: Philosophy (and, by the same token, metaphysics) is a discipline that requires mastery and practice, hard work and a commitment to methodological rigor.

HEGEL'S RESPONSE TO THE
KANTIAN CRITIQUE OF METAPHYSICS

There was much more to Hegel's agenda, as I have shown in the preceding chapters. But here, further dimensions must be considered as well. That Hegel was a systematic philosopher of the first order, committed to demonstrating the integrated organization of knowledge, is unquestionable. At the same time, it is vital to appreciate that his brand of speculative thinking marks a clear break with the metaphysical philosophies of the past. In this, Hegel owes much to his predecessor Immanuel Kant. In his *Critique of Pure Reason*, Kant argued that the only way to defeat skepticism and explain the reliability of knowledge is by positing that the mind structures sense experience in accordance with certain innate concepts or categories (cause, substance, thing, event, etc.).[7] The reason we can share knowledge about the world is that we all operate with the same knowing apparatus, which is responsible for imposing order on sensory input. Any form of thinking that extends such categories to objects that transcend experience is illegitimate and can only lead to bad results. Traditional rationalist metaphysicians did just this when they applied concepts pertaining to experience alone (cause, thing, permanence, etc.) to a shadow world of "reality-beyond-experience" that included entities (God, the soul, the world) that cannot be thought of and discussed without invoking concepts that are germane only to the context of perception. (Thus, for example, God is a substance and a cause, but to say so imports ideas proper to experience into discourse concerning an entity that transcends experience and therefore misapplies these ideas.) Kant maintained, in the end, not that metaphysics is impossible but that it must confine itself to the role of providing guidance for empirical investigation and drawing ultimate generalizations about the world from reflection upon the conceptual foundations of experience and the established laws of nature.

Kant's analysis of knowledge was revolutionary, and his critique of metaphysics was devastating. Because traditional metaphysics quested after a realm of being outside of experience, he concluded that the entire project of seeking rational knowledge of reality is doomed to failure. Reality is simply unknowable in his terms, for it cannot be described in principle. Metaphysicians of the past, therefore, had not only theorized in a groundless fashion, they were literally purveyors of nonsense. Not only this, but their reasonings had led them into paradoxes and into contradicting one another's conclusions. Now while Hegel recognizes the urgency of examining critically the concepts or categories that reason employs, he rejects Kant's ruling that metaphysics cannot formulate a meaningful and true overall view of reality. Hegel maintains instead that the highest truths to which we aspire are precisely discoverable in and through reflection *on* experience, and he disowns past metaphysicians' tendency to seek them by means of a leap into a supersensible, extramundane sphere. And in order to make good on this claim, he cautiously observes the need to develop a method of revealing reality from within the framework of thinking that is stimulated by, and constructs, experience. So Hegel veers away from Kant in making his own assertion that a type of ultimate knowledge is possible, and the reason he gives in support of this claim is that "the Absolute"— what we strive to know—is itself embedded in the world of experience.[8] We must find it there and set it forth in adequate concepts so that it will show itself in relief.

Hegel revamps metaphysics by interrogating its past assumptions (much like Kant) and setting off in a new direction. He does so by allowing thought to examine itself in action at each stage. Hegel's departure from previous modes of reflection upon reality is nicely summarized by Stephen Houlgate:

> The significant difference between [Hegel's] speculative philosophy and [traditional rationalist] metaphysics is that speculative philosophy challenges certain of the basic assumptions on which metaphysics is founded. It challenges the absolute distinctions between categories; it challenges the notion of a discrete subject distinct from its predicates and relations; and it even challenges the very notion of a foundation to philosophy itself.[9]

Whereas Kant saw the categories that govern experience as rigidly juxtaposed to one another, Hegel sees them as "dialectical"—as intimately connected, mutually dependent and mutually defining. Whatever is, is related to other things, and these relationships make it what it is (and makes them what they are). Finally, Hegel attempts to begin philosophizing without relying on presuppositions or foundational principles. The foregoing ideas, he thought, were the only ones that could free metaphysics to move beyond the restrictions imposed on it by Kant's critique.

INSIGHT AND INSPIRATION: DISCOVERING THE ABSOLUTE

What, then, *was* Hegel's vision? This is not difficult to locate, although it takes some patience to work through and comprehend it. There are, I think, two sides to the matter.

(1) In an early work, "Fragment of a System" (1800), Hegel wrote, "Life is the union of union and non-union."[10] This provides one clue we need; for as with life, so likewise with everything organic: It must be understood dialectically, as a uniting of opposites and a diversity that is also a unity. Since Hegel is a philosopher of process, he tends to see everything in terms of growth, development, transformation, decline, and rebirth (or regeneration), the characteristic phases through which living organisms pass. Hence, all features of reality, and reality as a whole, stand to be interpreted on an organic model, and reality too may be described as "the union of union and non-union." But is this more than just an unfathomable, Zen-koan type of utterance that confronts us with an air of mystery? The answer, of course, is yes: It represents what I identify as Hegel's fundamental vision. What we have here is not exactly an image, nor yet a clear conceptual claim. Rather, it is something more like a promissory note, the sketch of an idea, or, to use a computer analogy, the name of a file in which detailed information may be discovered, if one looks for it, or stored, if and when one finds it and formulates it in the required manner. In short, the statement has to be unpacked, and this is the task we now have before us.

A further clue to what Hegel meant by this apparently cryptic remark comes from viewing him as attempting to combine the basic insights of two ancient Greek philosophers, Heraclitus of Ephesus (fl. c. 500 BCE) and Parmenides of Elea (fl. c. 475 BCE). Hegel had enormous respect and admiration for the Pre-Socratics, among whom this pair of important and influential figures is numbered, and nearly two hundred pages of his monumental *Lectures on the History of Philosophy* are devoted to this group of early thinkers.[11] For our purposes it is sufficient to state that Heraclitus stood for the idea that reality is a restless flux and Parmenides, for the contrasting view that it is a changeless unity. If we join

these conceptions together, we get something like this: Reality is a multiplicity that can somehow be comprehended as a unity, a stable structure made up of individually mobile and unstable elements, where the
stability is to be found in the whole and the instability in the parts. It
might be observed, before we proceed further, that this is pretty much
the image of reality that we get from modern physics and cosmology—
another sign of Hegel's relevance to our contemporary world.[12]

Now in practical terms, how are these ideas to be united? As previous chapters have shown, the key to Hegel's method is that we must
first acknowledge that the world is permeated by opposing tendencies
of various sorts, and then apprehend the way in which these may be
"overcome" or "reconciled" by thought. In this dialectical procedure,
however, what we actually come to grasp, "thinkingly," is the structure
of reality itself—a rational whole made up of restless and discordant elements that, within the whole, are not (or at any rate, not ultimately) discordant. This is the meaning of one of Hegel's most memorable
remarks: "The true is thus the bacchanalian whirl in which no member
is not drunken; and because each, as soon as it detaches itself, dissolves
immediately—the whirl is just as much transparent and simple re-
pose."[13] Taken in isolation, our experiences of the world, and the concepts by means of which we mentally capture and digest them, are
wavering, fragile, and even a bit wild and crazy. But if we place them
under closer scrutiny and subject them to an ongoing and patient philosophical interrogation, we will eventually be able to gather together our
experiences and thoughts within a framework of understanding that is
durable and helps us fathom their most significant interconnections.
This same analysis also applies to historical, political, artistic, social,
and other forms of activity, where the parts make little sense on their
own but take on important meaning within a larger picture.

(2) In addition to positing this image of a dynamic matrix, Hegel
perceived reality in terms of an overarching divine or spiritual unity
("the Absolute"). His teaching is that the Absolute is always a presence
in our experience, however much it may be obscured by the immediate
objects of our care and concern. Moreover, the Absolute is always an
implicit (if not explicit) reference point for our thinking about the
world. Viewed from a slightly different angle, this means that *reality
exhibits an indwelling principle of intelligibility and cohesiveness*, which
becomes increasingly apparent as knowledge progresses to ever more
sophisticated levels. But beyond this, he is emphatic that *the actual sub-*

ject matter of metaphysics is the Absolute, as captured by one of a myriad "comprehendings," each of which is a particular act, focused on particular contents of consciousness that gain preeminence for us at a specific time and place. So, for instance, the notion of the Absolute as wholly other, unworldly, and transcendent, which Hegel dismisses in the preceding quotation, is a relatively crude, immature, and limited one compared to that which features its immanent presence and efficacy. Modern thought features the latter; earlier thought clings to the former.

Now what does it mean to assert that the Absolute is always "directly before us"? As many poets and naturalists record, what is of universal significance and value can be found by looking most deeply into the particular, which immediately confronts the eye. The macrocosm is present in the microcosm, infinity within finitude; the whole that we seek emerges from the part, wherein it has been concealed like a palimpsest. We can readily appreciate that this way of looking at things—which Hegel shares—seems to have more in common with Taoism or mysticism than with mainstream Western religions. It marks a significant departure from traditional Hebrew, Christian, and Islamic conceptions of the deity, an important theme to which I shall return.

Chapter 1 introduced Hegel's conception of philosophy as constituting a circular process. We are now in a position to acquire a greater understanding of what that signifies. Because the subject matter of philosophy is the Absolute, whose immanence in the world the inquiring intellect gradually reveals, and because the Absolute is "with us from the start," the result of philosophizing is implicit in the beginning and needs only to be drawn out.[14] Hence, Hegel writes: "The true is its own becoming, the circle that presupposes its end as its aim and thus has it for its beginning—that which is actual only through its execution and end."[15] Again, he returns to the image of circularity to explain the type of flow that is characteristic of rational thought as it generates results from within itself. Thought embraces its objects and interrogates them; out of this interaction emerge its findings, which represent what was potentially knowable in its objects and had lain awaiting discovery or realization through the act of knowledge.

Here, as elsewhere, Hegel argues that philosophical inquiry is "infinite." By this he means not that it goes on forever, never reaching a place to stop. Neither an infinite regress of explanations nor a series of results that stretches ad infinitum is a proper model for philosophy. Rather, as we've seen, the kind of thinking Hegel has in mind constitutes a circle, or rather, a circle of circles, an activity that leads to closure and completeness by returning to where it started from. Perhaps better put, philosophy enriches its initial postulates by developing them fully and extracting truth from them, but it does so from within the realm of thought, which overcomes its own limitations until there are none left needing to be overcome. Reality is then adequately assimilated and rendered in concepts. An infinite progression or regression of theories, explanations, or analyses Hegel refers to as "bad," "spurious," "wrong," or "negative" infinity; the self-liberating, all-embracing, circular movement of speculative philosophy he calls "good," "true," or "genuine" infinity.[16]

We can now see that for Hegel, knowledge of the Absolute is the goal we are perpetually trying to get at, the truth we elicit or attempt to tease out of whatever content we are momentarily concerned with. Many (if not most) of our attempts to know are false leads and errors that we must learn from and transcend toward something better. From the standpoint of the human species as well as from that of individual knowers, rationality only enters into our thought processes and achievements relatively late in the game. So the ultimate goal, argues our philosopher, is the cultivation of reason and the accumulation of its results within the framework of a disciplined, well-formed body of knowledge (which he calls "science"). Hegel states, more explicitly, that the conclusions metaphysical thinking produces "may be looked upon as definitions of the Absolute."[17] Whatever stage philosophical inquiry is at, then, it is always dealing with the Absolute in some guise, from some angle of attack, always homing in on the truth, the fullest conceptual expression of the Absolute that will be its eventual resting place. Consequently, ideas that are the currency of rational inquiry at any given point in time, however insubstantial or insufficient they may appear, are just so many ways of rendering the Absolute intelligible in the medium of thought. The goal of metaphysics is to unveil the presence of a rational principle at work in the world and to consolidate and integrate this knowledge into a coherent scheme of concepts that spells out this principle most clearly. "The Absolute," therefore, is in a sense merely the label Hegel attaches to reality, and when it is comprehensively and rationally understood, the organized system of knowledge obtained may be referred to as "absolute knowing."

THE PROBLEM OF THE STARTING POINT REVISITED

To summarize what we have established so far, we can say that Hegel's *method* of philosophizing transforms his *vision* into a set of results linked together to form a *system*. We can see more plainly what Hegel intended when referring to philosophy as a "system" if we examine a few more instances of how dialectical thinking operates and pushes us ever onward. In the *Phenomenology of Spirit* (as elsewhere), Hegel grapples with the problem of finding a starting point for thinking philosophically that does not make any unwarranted assumptions. This principle was first met in the opening pages of chapter 1. Now a dilemma at once presents itself to anyone proceeding in this manner. If we begin with raw (or "immediate") experience, it seems that knowledge cannot advance because this sensory input is merely chaotic or, as we might say, "inarticulate" or "incoherent." It finds no language in which to present its content. But if instead we start with experience that has already been organized to a certain extent by the mind ("mediated" by concepts, as Hegel puts it), then we violate the criterion to which we had committed ourselves, namely, that of avoiding unjustified presuppositions.[18] In several works, Hegel rehearses this perplexity, and rhetorically feigns despair: "a beginning, as primary and underived, makes an assumption, or rather is an assumption. It seems as if it were impossible to make a beginning at all."[19] How should we deal with this situation? Hegel suggests that rather than succumb to skepticism and self-defeat, we had better just get on with the job, maintaining our faith that the reasoning process in which we are engaged will eventually vindicate our starting point by the verdict of the results arrived at. And in doing so, it circles back to its own humble beginning to gather this up and make sense of it. This is why, as we have seen, it does not matter much where we start, as long as we do make a start of some kind. We must plunge in headlong and let the flow of thought carry us onward by its inner (dialectical) momentum, taking us where it will. While Hegel is confident that the final outcome will constitute a rational and total form of knowledge, he does not predict the course that thought will actually travel. This we must discover as we go along, learning by doing. Dialectical movement is nonlinear because there are always setbacks and backwaters of ignorance that have to be overcome as human endeavors push forward.

Hegel has great trust in our capacity to know. This is evident every-

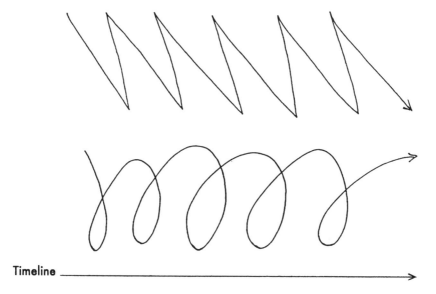

Timeline

Two models of dialectical progression.

where in his works. He does take skepticism and other challenges to knowing seriously, as we have learned. But part of his strategy is one of pretense: He tantalizes his readers with problems and leads them on. He himself is in no doubt as to the eventual outcome of philosophical inquiry, however, because he has already achieved the final results to which he alludes. So in effect, he is asking us to work with him through the same process he has previously undertaken and in that way to verify his findings. To make sure that we do, he adopts the artifice of bringing back to life the issues he earlier grappled with so that we can witness how the solutions to them unfold.

We might well ask, however, why we *should* follow Hegel in placing so much faith in the possibility of knowing the truth about reality. This kind of question brings us face-to-face with further complexities that concern knowledge and human cognition itself. Socrates and Plato early on identified a paradox that philosophers ever since have tried to resolve. It goes like this: If we ask ourselves what knowledge is, we find that it is very difficult to produce a satisfactory answer. But if it makes sense to seek a definition of the essence of knowledge at all, then we must be able to identify knowledge when we encounter it. However, if we can do *that*, then we must already possess knowledge of some kind and know what it is, for how else would we be able to recognize it? (Knowing what knowing is itself counts as a piece of knowledge.) It follows that we must "know before we know" or (more plainly put) that we must be able to rely on knowledge that we already have even in order to come to an understanding of what knowledge itself is. (Consider how odd it would sound for someone to make this assertion: "I can't tell you what knowledge is, but I know it when I see it.")

Subsequent thinkers have had a great deal of trouble defining knowledge, which has led many to wonder whether we do, in fact, have any at all. This issue passed through many permutations over the centuries until it was addressed by Kant, who decided that the capacity to know must be investigated and certified with the seal of philosophical approval before any reliable, far-reaching claims to know could be established. Hegel reacted by taking a new and different tack. As he rightly protests, "the examination of knowledge can only be carried out by an act of knowledge. To examine this so-called instrument is the same thing as to know it." He then adds, sardonically, "But to seek to know before we know [like Kant] is as absurd as the wise resolution of Scholasticus, not to venture into the water until he had learned to swim."[20] In other words, Hegel insists, *our knowing capacity must be granted the right to examine and certify itself*, for the ancient puzzle concerning what knowledge is will never be solved in any other way. What counts as knowing and what we can know will reveal themselves in due course, as thought investigates and corrects what it posits as true at each stage of its development.

DIALECTIC AT WORK: TWO EXAMPLES

Returning to the predicament of the starting point, we can now appreciate more clearly why Hegel declares that it makes little difference where we begin in philosophy. For what we will encounter is *self-instruction in the art of knowing*. Here is how it works. In the *Phenomenology of Spirit* Hegel challenges us to imagine (or some would say, "reenact") the drama of a first attempt to characterize the content of immediate sensory experience. In doing so, we take on the role of a hypothetical naive consciousness that has language but encounters the world for the first time.[21] An object is before us, but we cannot yet say or describe what it is; that would be an illegitimate overleaping of immediacy and would betray our thought-experiment. But if we are to articulate our experience at the most rudimentary level, what *can* we say about it? The suggestion is that we may only use language to *point* at the object, to single it out or put it on display, as it were, much as an ostensive definition of a word does (we define "red," for instance, by directing someone's attention to a red object). We could do this by employing terms like *this*, *here*, and *now*. Hegel then shows, however, having trapped his unwary reader, that while such words do succeed in picking out the *particular* object of our immediate experience by pointing to it, they are no less *universal* because they are transposable to an indefinite number of other contexts and different objects. When Hegel writes that "thinking is always the negation of what we have immediately before us," he conveys the idea that thought, by its natural endowment, marries particularity and universality and also extracts the latter from the former.[22] "To think the phenomenal [i.e., experiential] world . . . means to recast its form, and transmute it into a universal," he explains.[23] Thought, in other words, goes beyond the momentary and the particular by the very act of translating it into thought-contents—by ideation, conceptualizing, categorizing, and so forth. Then, by judging and criticizing its own products, it presses on to more adequate and lasting ideas about things. Insofar as words in our language perform the function of isolating individual referents, they are particular; insofar as they have generality of reference, they are universal. So one and the same word (such as *this*) both does and does not refer to what is before us, or to put it otherwise, it refers indifferently to whatever happens to be before us at any given moment. The upshot, according to Hegel, is that we are forced beyond the confines of the simplest concepts if we wish to characterize objects more fully and to reconcile the particularity and the universality we find in our consciousness of the world—even in the most rudimentary description of anything we discover through experience. (Eventually, when we possess better concepts and have become more thoughtful, we come to realize that what is individual or singular combines particularity with universality and is their union, the "concrete universal."[24])

The same lesson is extracted from a second example: knowledge of what a "thing" is.[25] A thing is, of course, something else (like knowledge) that we normally take for granted as understood by us. But when we approach the matter analytically or microscopically, we confront the fact that we do not really have such a good understanding after all.

Hegel's argument is that from the standpoint of untutored experiential consciousness (or what he calls "perception"), a thing is viewed as unitary, which, so far as it goes, is not incorrect. As an object, it is one and not many. Examined more carefully, however, a thing reveals itself as an unstable, internally contradictory entity. Why is this? The answer is that while a thing is just that—*a* thing or *an* object that is discrete—it is equally valid to regard it as a multiplicity of properties. That is, each thing owes its identity to a number of disparate aspects that it possesses and that make it what it is. But as we saw in chapter 2, everything that exists is constituted as much by the qualities it excludes from its nature as by the qualities it characteristically possesses. At a more refined level of analysis, then, we can say that each *quality* (such as colors, textures, shapes, and so on) is what it is both by *being* something (x, y, or z, etc.) and by *not-being* something else (a, b, or c, etc.). In relation to x, y, z, etc., other qualities it is *not* (a, b, c, etc.) are its negations or are "negated" by x, y, z, etc. (In like manner, of course, x, y, z, etc. are "negated" by a, b, c, etc.)

As we have gathered from the previous example, in which words like *this*, *here*, and *now* were considered as possible candidates for the job of describing raw experience, language, the means by which we convey our knowledge of the world, exhibits both particularity and universality at the same time, just as entities in the world do. Hegel contends that this creates instability in way we apprehend the collection of different properties that make up a thing. He reasons that each property, as instantiated, is a particular, but it is a universal too, so that the property, as it "inheres" in the thing, has a self-canceling or oscillating character exactly like that of *this*, *here*, and *now*. Any property we ascribe to a thing is both present in that thing *and* is a token of a type. (For example, this "red" is an instance of "redness"; this "big," an instance of "bigness"; etc.) Furthermore, each property "repels" every other alongside which it coexists because it asserts itself by not-being as much as by being. Each property is the "other" with respect to every different property, but its "otherness" plays a crucial role in defining, by juxtaposition, the qualities it opposes. Curiously, then, properties, which we think of as definite and distinct, are just as much connected by virtue of the fact that their distinctiveness is a function of oppositional pairings that define them. Each is the "other" of its opposite, so in a sense *the "other" is part of what every property is.*

Hegel does not leave the matter here, however. Nor does he engage

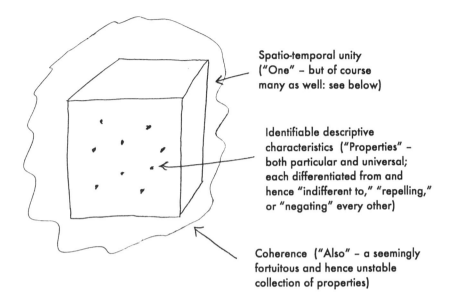

Spatio-temporal unity
("One" – but of course
many as well: see below)

Identifiable descriptive
characteristics ("Properties" –
both particular and universal;
each differentiated from and
hence "indifferent to," "repelling,"
or "negating" every other)

Coherence ("Also" – a seemingly
fortuitous and hence unstable
collection of properties)

A thing (according to the standpoint of "perception").

in denying the obvious: Whatever oddball philosophers may say, things really *are* separate entities. He acknowledges this by noting that the plurality of mutually negating properties that constitute a thing nevertheless coheres in some (as yet not understood) fashion. That is, the properties "hang together"—we know not how—and Hegel designates this elusive force of attraction, which seems like an occult power at this stage of inquiry, as the "also" feature of a thing. But the togetherness in which a thing's properties dwell represents an uneasy peace, with its unity ever threatened by the opposition among the properties.

We now have a thing analyzed in terms of *properties, also,* and *one,* where the first two somehow yield and account for the third. Because the unity of a thing is unstable, Hegel argues, we are forced ultimately to go beyond this level of analysis and description to embrace concepts and principles that express the inner dynamics of matter—among them the laws of nature—and then move on from these to the still-higher-order concepts that govern more adequate knowing of reality. This is much too elaborate a story to lay out fully here; it is, in fact, the remainder of Hegel's philosophical enterprise. Our immediate interest, in any event, lies only in the moral of the story: that limited forms of understanding push us of their own accord beyond themselves to more comprehensive forms, which, in turn, manifest *their* own defects, and so the process rolls onward.

Lest one be inclined to conclude that this is all merely the product of Hegel's fevered brain, it bears emphasis that the early careers of philosophy and science can be thought of as traveling a similar path to his, as I shall now try to show. Place yourself in the ancient world and consider the following hypothesis. Objects occupy space and hence are divisible. But if we persist in dividing them, we eventually reach a juncture beyond which we lack the physical means to divide still further. We can, however, continue *mentally* dividing and subdividing, and we can do so indefinitely. Therefore, matter, it seems, is endlessly (or infinitely) divisible into parts.[26] So we may decide to call a halt to this thought-experiment and posit the existence of a basic particle. The infinitesimally small part that we eventually reach in this fashion we may call an "atom." Now in order to explain why change occurs within and among objects, we may further suppose that there are many such atoms and that these are in constant motion.

We need not pursue this investigation any further, since it was only intended to suggest that this kind of reasoning, which was characteristic of the early Greek Atomists, Leucippus of Abdera (fl. c. 440 BCE) and Democritus of Abdera (fl. c. 420 BCE), is actually not at all unlike that of Hegel's naive consciousness, whose guise we have temporarily assumed. And we can also see that the same kind of dialectical impetus illustrated by Hegel pushed science beyond Atomism into later, more sophisticated formulations concerning the structure of matter. For the crude atomic theory just outlined leaves us wondering: How do any number of vanishingly small atoms, taken together, succeed in making up a solid object? What connects the atoms if they are constantly in motion? What orchestrates their movements so that they do not annihilate one another or the object that they constitute? Why can't they be further divided up anyway? And so on. Even today, we still have not solved all of these riddles, even though the theoretical pictures in which they reappear may have changed dramatically over time.

THE IDENTITY OF LOGIC AND METAPHYSICS

There is a further example of Hegel's practice of dialectical thinking I wish to discuss. In order to do so, some background on his notion of "logic" must be provided. In a sense that is peculiar to him, Hegel identifies *logic* and *metaphysics*.[27] The reason is that an investigation of the categories by means of which thought must proceed, and their necessary interrelationships, also yields a full characterization of reality itself. Consequently, he attempts, throughout the range of his works, to demonstrate that the same conclusions are arrived at whether thought engages with a particular field of interest or domain of human activity (philosophy of history, art, religion, etc.) or else conducts a more general schematic examination of its own skeletal apparatus or "thought forms" ("logic" proper). Hegel's identification of logic with metaphysics signals his plan to reveal, through the systematic arrangement of concepts, the rational structure of the real. To accomplish this, he seeks to show, first, that there are hitherto unappreciated or unsuspected logical links among the categories of thought itself. Second, in dealing with particular topics like history, politics, religion, the growth of experience, and so on, he demonstrates how in each subject of inquiry an inner necessity exhibits itself. The lesson to be learned is that thought distills out the rationality of experience in each of these areas. Thus, when Hegel does metaphysics, he is not making claims about what exists so much as defining how we should think about what exists.

Traditional metaphysicians often proposed and defended revised ontologies, that is, novel inventories of what exists (featuring Platonic Forms, God, monads, and other recondite entities). But unlike earlier thinkers, Hegel is not interested in portraying the world of experience merely as one of "appearance," behind which there sits an "ultimate reality." Quite the contrary: He may be seen as identifying and exploring the ontology he thinks we already have in place, and that has emerged in human consciousness with an implicit necessity that it is the job of philosophy to explain. This point can be clarified by means of a distinction derived from Kant: Hegel is not a "revisionist" metaphysician so much as a "descriptive" one.[28] That is, he does not recommend a new schema by which to conceive of what exists but rather tries to help us better understand what actually exists by rigorously analyzing how we think about fundamental aspects of the world. We must be careful, however, not to strip Hegel's metaphysics down to a mere shadow of itself, in the manner of some contemporary scholars who favor an interpretation of him that they style as "antimetaphysical." For Hegel remains wedded to certain ontological commitments (mainly to the existence of God and to dialectic as a force active in the world) that many would find unwarranted and objectionable. So while he is not a metaphysician of the sort that is excommunicated from the halls of philosophy by Kant, and while he respects Kantian criticism of speculative reason and has modified his own aspirations accordingly, he is a metaphysician nonetheless.

It follows, I believe, that a metaphysical/religious reading of Hegel is both justified and compelling. As we have seen in chapter 1, very significant disputes over the nature and interpretation of religion were raging in his time. These were a continuation of struggles that had been kindled by intellectual tendencies emerging out of the Renaissance and the Reformation and fueled by secularizing influences that stemmed from the rise of science, the Industrial Revolution, and various political theories and events. It is one thing to enlist a thinker such as Hegel in support of a modern philosophical agenda or movement (say, postmodernism) but quite another to sever him from his historical and ideological context. Reappropriating cultural contributions of the past so as to update their relevance is a healthy thing, but we must always keep in mind the sorts of issues to which they were originally a response. In Hegel's case, the loss of God was a vital cultural possibility he wished to combat: One of his most poignant sketches is that of the "unhappy consciousness," striving for union with a remote deity,[29] and a two-hundred-plus-page appendix to his three-volume *Lectures on the Philosophy of Religion* is devoted to resurrecting the traditional proofs of God's existence in the wake of Kant's withering critique of them.[30]

DIALECTIC AT WORK: A THIRD EXAMPLE

For an additional illustration of dialectical thinking in practice, we will look at the way in which Hegel's logic begins. Because his conception of logic is so basic to his entire philosophical enterprise, this example will facilitate a better understanding of his system as a whole. In both his massive *Science of Logic* and in his smaller *Encyclopedia Logic* (from which I have quoted numerous times), Hegel begins in the manner described earlier, that is, by adopting a position that entails minimal or no ontological or epistemological commitments.[31] To make this proce-dure more intelligible, suppose that someone were to ask you the fol-lowing question: "Tell me quickly—what's the most basic feature of the world (or of reality)?" The answer Hegel anticipates is simply: "*It is.*" In other words, the world has *being.* This statement not only seems indis-putable but also might reasonably be assumed to be the necessary departure for any discourse about the world. (If the world *is not,* then there is no subject matter to be concerned with—indeed there are also no persons to entertain concerns about it!) Hence, we may take Being as our initial, simplest, most barren category of thought about the world. Hegel then has us share with him the reflection that Being, if we try to get ahold of it conceptually, slips away into *nothingness*; it has pre-cisely zero content. To pin it down in thought is like trying to grab a ghost. It follows, he urges, that "Being" is indistinguishable from "Nothing," our second category.

In different terms, to characterize the world by applying the concept "Being" to it is to say nothing at all about it. (It is completely uninfor-mative to be told merely that the world *is.*) So far so good. But, Hegel points out and encourages us to note in ourselves, when Being slides into Nothing, there is a noticeable *movement of thought* that is taking place, and this gives us a sense of change that we may label "Becoming," our third category. The world is characterized by its transitory quality, and in this manner we must also think about it, he believes. But becoming, we've noted, is both being and not-being (or nothing) rolled into one. Something that is becoming—that is underway toward assuming another state or undergoing transformation—both is (what it moves away from) and is-not (what it passes into). From a slightly dif-ferent perspective, we can see that when a change occurs, the thing undergoing alteration is not yet what it will be, nor is it entirely what it was; it's somewhere in between—in transit, as it were. Becoming is the concept Hegel uses to capture this movement that resides at the heart of existence, which forces itself upon our attention at even the most rudimentary level of thought and experience.

With reference to thought, "Becoming" names the corrosive dy-namic of self-negation that dwells within all concepts and manifests itself in our simplest formulations about the world. Not only does each thing or state of affairs come to be and pass away into something else, so too does each of our concepts give way to others that supplant ear-lier cognitive constructions and determine the path of further inquiry.

In conceptual terms, then, "Becoming" transforms "Being" and "Nothing" into a new unity of thought because thought is always in contact with, and trying to understand, a changing world.

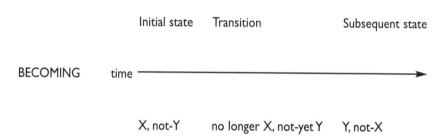

The flow of becoming: Any object of inquiry undergoes change from how we first characterize it (X) to how we later do (Y).

Hegel cleverly ties in the dialectic of Being-Nothing-Becoming with two other themes he holds dear. One is the now familiar idea of a pre-suppositionless starting point. Thus, he notes that whatever we call a "Beginning" is both a "Being" and a "Nothing," too. Why is this? Hegel answers that it is because "In its beginning, the thing is not yet, but it is more than merely nothing. For its Being is already in the beginning."[32] In brief, something that is just getting underway—whether an event, an argument, a new life, and such—must have some properties, however slight, to *be* at all, but from the standpoint of where it is heading, it is void of other properties. It both is and is-not. By implication, a starting point (for example, in philosophy) is both an assertion and an emptiness; it signifies both a first movement and the absence of any concrete result having been obtained as yet. Furthermore, to become something, an entity must have the potential to be that something. And this potential it possesses from the outset (therefore, "its Being is already in the beginning").

The second theme that hovers in the background here is Hegel's thesis that our ideas eventually will be in harmony with reality, showing it to be a rational order. As I pointed out earlier, this does not mean that a novel picture of the world will replace our ordinary one; rather, we shall come to learn that we already have some, and can derive the rest, of the concepts we need in order to make the world thoroughly comprehensible. Making good on such a claim is a tall order, but Hegel never shies away from his commitment to this principle.

Many have suspected that these reflections on Being, Nothing, and Becoming contain some kind of sleight-of-hand maneuver. Hegel foresees this worry, however, and comments, "No great expense of wit is needed to ridicule the proposition that being and nothing are the same, or rather to produce absurdities which are falsely asserted to be the consequences and applications of this proposition; e.g., that, on that view, it is all the same whether my house, my fortune, the air to breathe, this city, the sun, the law, the spirit, God, *are* or *are not*." But, as he quickly adds, this is "just business as usual for the unthinking mind."[33] We must remember that his thought-experiment is intended only to help philosophical inquiry get off the ground, and it nicely illustrates the way in which ideas have a life and energy of their own, ever changing into their opposites and pushing us beyond limits to new ideas of more encompassing richness. Hegel asserts,

> If the logical forms of the Concept were really dead, inactive, and indifferent receptacles of representations or thoughts, then, as far as truth is concerned, our information about them would be a completely superfluous and dispensable *description*. In fact, however, being forms of the Concept they are, on the contrary, *the living spirit of what is actual*; and what is true of the actual is only *true in virtue of these forms, through them* and *in them*.[34]

The categories arrived at by metaphysical reasoning are not abstract and empty, in other words; they are the vital expression of what is real, which naturally manifests itself in the medium of thought. (Hegel insists, still more radically, that the process of deriving these categories is what *makes* reality complete its evolution into what it had the potential of becoming, namely, a rational whole, known to be such. We shall revisit this claim in chapter 4.)

How should we apply Hegel's ideas about the logical forms of thought? If we grant him that Being is a justifiable entry point into the categorial scheme by means of which we structure the world, and that Being is empty of content, we can then follow his line of reasoning that leads us to Becoming. Once having got *there*, it is not difficult to allow, as he wishes us to do, that Being must take on *some* properties (must *become* something, in other words) in order to be known in a definite form. Thus emerges in consciousness the structure of the world we know.

A parallel to this movement between pure thought categories can be discovered in the history of philosophy, Hegel shows us.[35] Leaving aside the precise chronological order of their appearance on the stage of the ancient past, he charts a dialectical clash of the following sort, using Heraclitus and Parmenides as his metaphysical foils. Parmenides identified unchangeable, featureless Being with the cosmos. This was a hollow conception (indistinguishable from Nothing). From a Heraclitean standpoint, its vacuousness is evident, and therefore an opposing idea suggests itself: that of flux or ceaseless change (Becoming) as the primordial principle. But while this represents an advance in thinking, Heraclitus's view ran into its own problems, since a vision of pure becoming repels any attribution of stable properties to reality. Therefore, as Hegel argues, further developments were called for in order to arrive at a more satisfactory ontology. In general terms, he asserts that thought finds itself forced beyond mere Becoming to "Determinate Being," its next category. The remainder of Hegel's logical (or metaphysical) exercise coalesces around the question, What must the world (or reality) be like in order for us to talk about it all, to think about it intelligently, and ultimately to make sense of it? Hegel's response is to delineate different kinds of "determinate being" until he thinks reality is completely and adequately characterized. How does he know when this goal has been reached? In order to answer this question, we need to focus more closely on what Hegel meant by a "system."

THE SYSTEM

Chapter 1 highlighted Hegel's organic conception of the history of philosophy. The reader will recall that the truth, as Hegel sees it, issues slowly from a long and painstaking (indeed, painful) process to which many have contributed—through their faults as much as through their more positive and durable achievements. Hegel maintains that the many and diverse philosophical efforts of the past, gathered together under the rubric "history of philosophy," represent perspectives or standpoints that have something to contribute to an overall understanding of reality, but because they are partial in one way or another, they fall short of adequacy. What *would* yield an adequate outlook? And what does "adequate" mean, in this context? Hegel speaks very directly to this matter when he writes, "It is erroneous to understand by 'system' a philosophy whose principle is restricted and [kept] distinct from other principles; on the contrary, it is the principle of genuine philosophy to contain all particular principles within itself."[36] This statement bears an absolutely indelible Hegelian trademark. By making it, Hegel adopts a position I am tempted to describe, only a little facetiously, as "anti-'ism'-ism," for he presents himself as the archfoe of warring factions in philosophy. What is really going on here? The answer is that he is expressing the desire to introduce into the clangorous diversity of past philosophies an overarching principle of unity, with the ultimate aim of transforming apparent chaos into conceptual harmony. In this manner, he hopes to break out of the circle of "isms" and schisms that have infected human thought and sapped the energies of the best minds since the beginning of recorded thought. Hegel's concern is clearly sounded in the following passage:

> Unless it is a system, a philosophy is not a scientific production. Unsystematic philosophizing can only be expected to give expression to personal peculiarities of mind, and has no principle for the regulation of its contents. Apart from their independence and organic union, the truths of philosophy are valueless, and must be treated as baseless hypotheses, or personal convictions. Yet many philosophical treatises confine themselves to such an exposition of the opinions and sentiments of the author.[37]

That Hegel himself sought to escape from this bind should by now be quite evident.

As we are coming to learn, a system is an organized totality of thought, a cognitive construct that embraces all limited positions and emerges out of them as their most comprehensive expression and fulfillment. Hegel is quite adamant that we appreciate his stance in the correct spirit, and he goes to considerable lengths to justify and embellish his argument. In the following passage, he summarizes his point clearly and forcefully: "Opinion considers the opposition of what is true and false quite rigid, and, confronted with a philosophical system, it expects agreement or contradiction. And in an explanation of such a system, opinion still expects to find one or the other. It does not comprehend the difference of the philosophical systems in terms of the progressive development of the truth, but sees only the contradiction in this difference."[38] I have previously called attention to the kind of holistic process Hegel describes here. It was equated in chapter 2 with the emergence of a new product in a chemical reaction. We also saw there that he uses the metaphor of a plant's growth phases to convey the sort of continuous development he sees as a general feature, not only of changes taking place in the world, but also, more specifically, of the historical accumulation of knowledge. People *do* tend to adopt an "either/or" approach to philosophers' views, assuming that one must choose whether to be a Platonist or an Aristotelian, a Rationalist or an Empiricist, a Modernist or a Postmodernist, and so on.[39] But according to Hegel, this is a profound mistake. There is a current of insights that may be traced over time and through the intricate web of opposing— partially false, partially true—positions and that issues finally as the full truth he strives to articulate within his own system.[40] So while there *is* genuine conflict among philosophical standpoints, this is only part of the story; more importantly, there is also the underlying matrix of understanding, which each view helps build by means of the accretions it leaves behind. Skirmishes among philosophers manifest the turmoil and creative energy that cause advances to take place. Each position actively (but unwittingly) helps liberate the cognitive potential of every other. It is as legitimate to say, then, that philosophical positions are connected as that they are separate and distinct—even more so, if Hegel is right. For he holds that the objective of a *complete* philosophy is to subsume all of its competing predecessors, digesting and re-presenting their diverse "principles" in an overarching worldview.

TRANSCENDING KANT'S POSITION

To construct such a philosophy is a stupendously ambitious plan, as Hegel well realizes. But an understanding of his project tells us why he felt compelled to write not only a philosophical history of philosophy but also a comprehensive treatise on every other major subject of concern to the discipline. Although we cannot unfold such an undertaking without rewriting Hegel's system, we can at least gain an idea of the procedure he follows. As I indicated earlier in this chapter, Hegel attempted to fuse (and by doing so, to transcend) the standpoints of Heraclitus and Parmenides. This provides one instance of how he dialectically subsumes and surpasses past philosophers. Another illustration can be found in his relationship to the classical phase of Rationalism and Empiricism and to the Kantian Critical Philosophy. The essential principle of Rationalism, historically, was that unaided reason is capable of obtaining knowledge *independently of experience* that is both substantive and certain. The central idea of Empiricism was that all reliable substantive knowledge comes precisely *from experience*. As well, Rationalists held that some of our most general ideas are innate. Empiricists denied this, arguing that even these are abstracted in some fashion from original experiences. Kant responded to this conflict between philosophical schools by partly endorsing, partly rejecting the alternatives presented by each and thereby broke an epistemological logjam. He accepted the position that all knowledge *begins* with experience but added that this does not mean that it is totally *derived from* experience. While sense perception arouses our capacity for knowing, we can only know what our inborn mental apparatus enables us to know.[41] Hence, experience impinges upon us and provides sensory input, but the concepts supplied by the mind account for the structure imposed upon these data. Without this activity of the mind, we would have no information, only a bombardment of raw, unfiltered, meaningless stimuli. Knowledge, then, is a product of experience plus conceptual ordering. In arriving at his conclusion, therefore, Kant dialectically "absorbed" the principles of Rationalism and Empiricism and went beyond them to fashion a new epistemology.

Hegel approved of this line of reasoning but judged that Kant had not gone far enough. For one thing, Kant postulated a somewhat arbitrary and incomplete set of concepts (or "categories") as constituting the mind's innate endowment. Hegel believed that concepts have to be produced out of the mind's own self-development and vindicated by it, as we've seen. Kant also left behind an unresolved dichotomy between the knowable phenomena of experience and so-called things-in-themselves, composing the unknowable, fugitive world that allegedly lies beyond experience and causes it to occur. Hegel, like many post-Kantian thinkers, found this totally unsatisfactory. (Recall his argument against limits that cannot be transcended, which was outlined in chapter 1.) Finally, as we have seen, Kant's opinion was that our ability to know had to justify itself before any knowing could take place. To Hegel, this was absurd; the mind defines its powers through discerning the successes and failures of its own previous acts of cognition. (Since human rationality is what it does, it learns what it can do by doing it.)

Kant's views were flawed because they were riddled with contradictions that had not been properly addressed and overcome. He is not to be blamed, however, since this is a natural and regularly recurring stage of thought's evolution. To a certain extent, Kant realized that his views were problematic, but rather than endorse contradiction, he regarded it as the dead end and death knell of reasoning. Hegel's self-assigned task, then, was to assimilate and transcend Kant's view, which also meant to envelop and surpass those positions that Kant himself had subsumed and to appropriate and process the contradictions that had stymied his great predecessor. To advance beyond Kant, Hegel trained his attention on keeping thought and experience in intimate contact, each validating and reinforcing the other while at the same time maturing in relation to it. Furthermore, as already mentioned several times, thought discovers, in and through the analysis of experience, the rational structure of reality. Experience and thought become inseparable, and there is no crevice that can develop into a split between them.

As we see here, Hegel's goal was to heal the rift between the knower and the known that had haunted philosophy since its earliest days. How can the mind really know the world? How can the mental or spiritual make contact with the physical and indifferent other, with nature, with material objects? Hegel's quest was to find a means of surmounting this dualism. He believed he had discovered it in the dialectical process whereby rational thought transcends its barriers and, through self-discipline, orders what can be known into a seamless system. (As an idealist, we will recall, he holds that "the world" is what is known to us and sorted out within consciousness.)

The last stage reached by Hegel's philosophizing is "absolute knowledge" or, more actively, "absolute knowing." It would be a mistake to suppose, however, that this means the capstone of his system must be some new and utterly different kind of attainment. Instead, what he tells us is that the final step thought takes is to comprehend the Absolute as both the complex matrix of knowledge that the rational intellect has constructed during its laborious historical voyage *and* as the way things are—the whole of reality of which we, as individual thinkers and doers, are constitutive parts. This wider worldview is the core of Hegel's "metanarrative," "grand narrative of legitimation," or "theodicy."[42] In the next two chapters, on the Absolute and truth, we will have a closer look at how Hegel achieves his ultimate design.

NOTES

1. Aristotle, *Metaphysics*, in *The Basic Works of Aristotle*, ed. Richard McKeon, trans. W. D. Ross (New York: Random House, 1941), bk. 1, 980a, 982b, pp. 689, 692.

2. F. H. Bradley, *Appearance and Reality: A Metaphysical Essay* (London: Swan Sonnenschein; New York: Macmillan, 1893), p. xiv. Bradley (1846–1924), an original and significant metaphysician in his own right, was the leading member of the so-called British Idealist movement that flourished briefly at the turn of the twentieth century.

3. G. W. F. Hegel, preface to *Philosophy of Right*, trans. T. M. Knox (Oxford: Clarendon Press, 1945), p. 7.

4. G. W. F. Hegel, *Phenomenology of Spirit*, trans. A. V. Miller (Oxford: Clarendon Press, 1977), secs. 69, 70, p. 43.

5. G. W. F. Hegel, "With What Must the Science Begin?" in *The Science of Logic*, trans. A. V. Miller (London: Allen and Unwin; New York: Humanities Press, 1969), p. 67 (emphasis in original). The undisclosed but specific reference here is to Friedrich von Schelling (1775–1854), Hegel's contemporary former philosophical ally and later philosophical foe.

6. G. W. F. Hegel, *Encyclopaedia Logic*, trans. T. F. Geraets, W. A. Suchting, and H. S. Harris (Indianapolis: Hackett, 1991), sec. 5, p. 28.

7. Immanuel Kant, *The Critique of Pure Reason*, trans. Norman Kemp Smith (London: Macmillan; New York: St. Martin's Press, 1956). This work was originally published in 1781, with a second edition appearing in 1787.

8. God, or the subject of Hegel's vision. See below and chapter 4 for a full exposition.

9. Stephen Houlgate, *Hegel, Nietzsche and the Criticism of Metaphysics* (Cambridge: Cambridge University Press, 1983), p. 123.

10. G. W. F. Hegel, "Fragment of a System," in *The Hegel Reader*, ed. Stephen Houlgate, trans. Richard Kroner (Oxford: Blackwell, 1998), p. 36. This "Fragment" can also be found in G. W. F. Hegel, *Early Theological Writings*, trans. T. M. Knox and Richard Kroner (Chicago: University of Chicago Press, 1948), pp. 309–19.

11. G. W. F. Hegel, *Lectures on the History of Philosophy*, trans. E. S. Haldane and Frances H. Simson, vol. 1 (New York: Humanities Press, 1963), pp. 165–349.

12. See Stephen Hawking, *The Universe in a Nutshell* (New York: Random House, 2001).

13. See Hegel's preface to *Phenomenology of Spirit*, in *Hegel: Texts and Commentary*, trans. Walter Kaufmann (Notre Dame, IN: University of Notre Dame Press, 1977), p. 424. See also Hegel, *Phenomenology of Spirit*, trans. Miller, sec. 47, p. 27.

14. To say "only" here is a bit misleading, for we must bear in mind that the process so described is a laborious and frustrating (but eventually rewarding) one, in Hegel's view.

15. *Hegel: Texts and Commentary*, trans. Kaufmann, p. 388; Hegel, *Phenomenology of Spirit*, trans. Miller, sec. 18, p. 10.

16. See either G. W. F. Hegel, *Hegel's Logic*, trans. William Wallace, 3rd ed. (Oxford: Clarendon Press, 1975), secs. 93–95, or Hegel, *Encyclopaedia Logic*, secs. 93–95. See also M. J. Inwood, *Hegel* (London: Routledge and Kegan Paul, 1983), pp. 364–66, where seven different ways in which Hegel believed thought to be infinite are explained.

17. Hegel, *Encyclopaedia Logic*, sec. 85, p. 135.

18. Hegel explains mediation in general terms: "For to mediate is to take something as a beginning and go onward to a second thing; so that the existence of this second thing depends on our having reached it from something else contradistinguished from it." (*Hegel's Logic*, sec. 12, p. 17.) Elsewhere, he supplements this somewhat abstract account with helpful examples: "immediate *existence* is bound up with its mediation. The seed and the parents are immediate and initial existences in respect of the offspring which they generate. But the seed and the parents, though they exist and are therefore immediate, are yet in their turn generated; and the child, without prejudice to the mediation of its existence, is immediate, because it *is*. The fact that I am in Berlin, my immediate presence here, is mediated by my having made the journey hither." *Hegel's Logic*, sec. 66, p. 102 (emphases in original).

19. Hegel, *Hegel's Logic*, sec. 1, p. 3.

20. Ibid., sec. 10, p. 14. Wallace tells us that "Scholasticus" is the name of a fictional character whose exploits were used in the instruction of Greek schoolboys by Hierocles, a follower of Pythagoras of Samos (fl. c. 530 BCE). See Hegel, *Hegel's Logic*, translator's note to the passage just cited, p. 298.

21. Whether this epistemological pretense is at all plausible has been the subject of much controversy, even among Hegel scholars. See, for example, Jacob Loewenberg, *Hegel's "Phenomenology": Dialogues on the Life of Mind* (La Salle, IL: Open Court, 1965), Dialogue 2. Hegel's naive consciousness of "sense-certainty" is portrayed in *Phenomenology*, trans. Miller, secs. 90–110, pp. 58–66.

22. Hegel, *Hegel's Logic*, sec. 12, p. 17.

23. Ibid., sec. 50, p. 81.

24. Ibid., or Hegel, *Encyclopaedia Logic*, secs. 163–64.

25. Hegel, *Phenomenology*, trans. Miller, secs. 111–31, pp. 67–79.

26. This progression yields another example of what Hegel would call the "bad" infinite.

27. Hegel, *Hegel's Logic*, or *Encyclopaedia Logic*, sec. 24.

28. See P. F. Strawson, *Individuals: An Essay in Descriptive Metaphysics*

(London: Methuen, 1959), introduction. Strawson remarks that "Metaphysics has often been revisionary, and less often descriptive. Descriptive metaphysics is content to describe the actual structure of our thought about the world, revisionary metaphysics is concerned to produce a better structure" (p. 9).

29. Hegel, *Phenomenology*, B, IV, B (trans. Miller, secs. 206–30, pp. 126–38).

30. G. W. F. Hegel, "Lectures on the Proofs of the Existence of God," in *Lectures on the Philosophy of Religion*, vol. 3, pp. 155–367.

31. Hegel, *Science of Logic*, chap. 1; Hegel, *Hegel's Logic* or *Encyclopaedia Logic*, secs. 86–88.

32. Hegel, *Hegel's Logic*, sec. 88, p. 130.

33. Hegel, *Encyclopaedia Logic*, sec. 88, pp. 141, 142 (emphases in original).

34. Ibid., sec. 162, p. 239 (emphases in original).

35. Hegel, *Lectures on the History of Philosophy*, vol. 1, pt. 1, sec. 1, chap. 1; Hegel, *Science of Logic*, pp. 83–93.

36. Hegel, *Encyclopaedia Logic*, sec. 14, p. 39.

37. Hegel, *Hegel's Logic*, sec. 14, p. 20.

38. See *Hegel: Texts and Commentary*, trans. Kaufmann, p. 370, or Hegel, *Phenomenology of Spirit*, trans. Miller, sec. 2, p. 2.

39. Because I teach Existentialism, I am often asked whether I am an Existentialist—apparently on the assumption that you naturally exemplify the position you teach about. If you don't, then you are opposed to it and disdain to teach about it. (You are either for X or against X, and there's no ground in between.)

40. Hegel does indeed hold that falsity is an element of the truth. This odd-sounding doctrine (discussed in detail in chapter 5) has a threefold meaning. First, as we have already seen, truth must be understood as a process, not merely as a static state of affairs or sterile result taken in isolation from the pathway by which it was attained. Second, limited or partial standpoints (that is, any philosophical positions that fall short of the all-inclusiveness Hegel ascribes to his own view) are "one-sided" because they promote a particular perspective or agenda and exhibit what we would nowadays call "tunnel vision." Such positions therefore are partly true, partly false; yet if they contribute to the whole story philosophy has to tell (as Hegel believes they do), this story "contains" both the true and the false aspects of the individual positions that it embraces and builds upon. Third, Hegel allows that there are degrees of truth. This entails that the later stages of the process through which the story of philosophy unfolds are "truer" than the earlier ones and that the final development in the temporal sense (Hegel's own view) is the "truest" in the logical sense as well, or at any rate has the greatest claim to have captured the entire truth.

41. Kant, *Critique of Pure Reason*, B1–B6, pp. 41–45.

42. The terms "metanarrative" and "grand narrative of legitimation" were introduced by Jean-François Lyotard in "The Postmodern Condition," in *After Philosophy: End or Transformation?* ed. Kenneth Baynes, James Bohman, and Thomas McCarthy (Cambridge, MA: MIT Press, 1987), pp. 73–94. The term "theodicy" belongs to the traditional vocabulary of philosophy and religious studies and refers to a justification of the ways of God, or of God's goodness, taking the existence of evil into account.

4

THE ABSOLUTE

A PHILOSOPHER OF THE SPIRIT

Like other elements of his thought, Hegel's weltanschauung, or worldview, has led a checkered career. While once attractive to many, it has also sparked controversy, heated rejection, and even ridicule. This makes it all the more intriguing to examine, but also all the more precarious to explain and evaluate. A good scholarly approach to a philosopher's work should always attempt first to record accurately what he or she said and only then to engage in criticism. Observing this principle is probably more important in relation to the present topic than it is to any other aspect of interpreting Hegel.

Hegel has been viewed as many things: social theorist, political philosopher, bourgeois ideologist, proto-Fascist, systematic metaphysician, philosophical historian, forerunner of the phenomenological movement, anti-foundationalist precursor to postmodernism—the list goes on. But whatever else we might say of him, I believe he was deeply committed to a religious outlook, as I have made plain in chapter 3. We have to be careful how we interpret his position, however, because although he often tried to integrate Christian doctrines into his theories, arguing that Christianity was the most complete form of religion, and attributing special importance to the Christian era in the realization of human freedom, he was much more than an apologist or proselytizing theologian in disguise. Furthermore, parts of his work can be read and evaluated outside of a religious framework. But because Hegel cautions us not to approach his philosophy piecemeal, we cannot really escape his religious orientation, even if we wanted to.

Hegel had a conventional Lutheran upbringing and studied theology at the University of Tübingen in southern Germany, yet he became, if anything, a maverick or eccentric religious thinker. There are three main grounds for this assessment. First, in his mature writings he expresses the conviction that philosophy, because it comprehends religion and subsumes its insights in the form of pure concepts freed from bondage to images and symbols, surpasses religion and becomes the highest human attainment. (For similar reasons, he thought philosophy ascends above art as well.) Second, in order to force us to think philosophically, he prefers to speak of "the Absolute" rather than of "God" so that preconceptions of the deity will drop away and not encumber inquiry. Third, Hegel's Absolute is *both transcendent* (greater than the world, inexhaustible) *and immanent* (at work in, and in some sense identical with, the rhythm of the world). This idea has been condemned as heretical throughout the painful history of world religion. Given these qualifications, it might be preferable to call Hegel a "spiritual" philosopher, which we may keep in mind as a useful alternative.[1] This choice is reinforced by the fact that he often speaks of "Spirit" (in German, *Geist*, often and less correctly translated as "Mind") when referring to human endeavors and "Absolute Spirit" (interchangeably with "the Absolute") when designating the principle of divine rationality that animates activities in the world and encompasses Spirit in the more limited, mundane, human sense.

For Hegel, Spirit has a destiny, and Absolute Spirit has an "essence" to actualize and manifest. To get to the core of these ideas requires that we focus on the key concepts that have just been introduced. Spirit is the common consciousness of humankind in which we all participate and that evolves over time. In everyday life, we frequently employ expressions like "the spirit of the time," "the spirit of a people," or "the human spirit," and when we do, we come close to Hegel's meaning. Hegel sees humanity as a community of knowers and doers that stretches across time and space so that the accomplishments of individuals, in coming to a greater understanding of the world, contribute to the advancement of our entire species toward that goal. Whether we are aware of their influence, breakthroughs in knowledge and even inroads of a very small order constantly move us forward both cognitively and practically. Thomas Edison's inventions, the product of one mind, have had vast repercussions and are used by us daily. Albert Einstein's discoveries are fully intelligible to only a few individuals, yet their impact is experienced by us all, in terms of the nuclear weapons and nuclear energy that they make possible, and no doubt in many ways yet to be discerned, such as limitations on space and time travel. Some totally unknown person who learns how to multiply still further the capacity of microchips, or to replace them altogether, unleashes a new computer revolution that transforms yet again the way we communicate. Most generally, Hegel would say that whatever idea or creative result anyone produces becomes the property of all (and, we might add, laws on "intellectual property" notwithstanding). A Pablo Picasso, a Nelson Mandela, a Toni Morrison, or a Jane Goodall changes the way we look at the world, live in it, and project ourselves toward the future. For better or worse, we are all in the same boat, all realizing parts of the potential of humanity, or of Spirit, as Hegel would affirm. And so it is not only the famous individuals who make such an impact. As social critic Charles A. Reich states, "No person's gain in wisdom is diminished by anyone else's gain. . . . Indeed, each man, his experiences, his personality, his uniqueness, becomes an asset to other men when their object is to gain in wisdom. Each person, by practicing his own skills, pursuing his own interests, and having his own experiences becomes of increasing value to others."[2] Contemporary botanist William H. Murdy reinforces the point, noting, "In large measure, our personalities are determined by a collective consciousness which we can contribute to and which is itself evolving."[3]

What is Spirit's target, toward which human achievements, knowingly or unknowingly, direct their energies? Hegel thinks it is one of comprehending the process whereby human consciousness attains to self-understanding. That is, he believes consciousness completes its vocation when it reaches the point at which its own origin, progression, and fruitful productivity are amalgamated into a single thought pattern that reveals the significance of it all. This he regards as the highest development of reflective self-consciousness and it takes place, he argues, within philosophy's domain. Consciousness emerges out of originally unconscious nature. Over time, self-consciousness arises out of consciousness and becomes capable of inquiring about the process by means of which it has itself arisen, the path it has traveled, and where it is heading. Hegel's notion is that this is the ultimate fulfillment of thought—to ask and answer these questions. Once having answered them, it achieves its ultimate end, or "actualizes" itself most completely. His special way of expressing all of this is to say that consciousness first "externalizes" itself by investigating its natural origins (its dormant or nascent presence in nature), experiencing in this process its own "self-estrangement" or "otherness." Then, in coming to understand its own development out of nature and eventually into what it has become over time, namely, human self-consciousness, it "overcomes its alienation," "returns to itself out of its other," or "negates its negation." Finally, it becomes "at home in itself" by having taken this journey because by doing so, consciousness realizes its own *telos* or actualizes its "inner principle," its drive to achieve self-understanding through self-mastery and self-expression. By projecting itself outward and actively disclosing the intelligible fabric of the world, thought makes itself identical with being, which no longer opposes it as lying beyond comprehension in whole or in part.

CONSCIOUSNESS EVOLVING

As it retraces this process of self-emergence, consciousness writes its own anthropological autobiography or psychobiography. We have seen that consciousness learns it has evolved naturally, but it also discovers that it has served as the vehicle for humans' emancipation from total dependency on nature.[4] Higher-order consciousness, for Hegel as for many other philosophers, marks the distinction between humans and other organisms, and this is largely because it serves as the vehicle for liberation—first of all, from the condition of animal subservience to basic needs, and much later, from political domination by other humans. How consciousness arises initially is not something upon which Hegel dwells, but this is not a gap peculiar to his account, since the emergence of consciousness remains a fundamental mystery even today. Be this as it may, consciousness expresses its highest development in the form of *self*-consciousness, and Hegel has a good deal to say about how *this* result comes about, which I consider below. "Self-consciousness," in the sense used here, refers not only to the awareness of being a self but also to the reflexive acts in which consciousness examines and assesses its own operations. Specifically with regard to the second of these meanings, human consciousness reaches its developmental goal, for Hegel, when it surveys and comprehends the evolution to full capacity of its own uniquely rational powers. Thus, the "destiny" of consciousness (as I am calling it) is *to know itself in the act of knowing, to thinkingly understand the pathway and pattern of its own emergence*. A reasonably accurate characterization of Hegel's entire philosophical endeavor, then, is that it concerns the free and fluid movement of consciousness toward this end-state. While the process is most explicitly laid out in the *Phenomenology of Spirit*, it nevertheless remains the explicit or implicit subject of all his other works as well. Consciousness, in its most advanced form as *self*-consciousness, undergoes a laborious and perilous voyage of exploration. This is a journey in which it discloses to itself its own way of coming to be, continuing to evolve in the very same act and beyond, steadily unfolding its full potential.

The idea that we naturally seek to actualize our human capacities most completely is both old and new. Aristotle subscribed to the belief that organic development follows a trajectory from potentiality to actuality. A living being, observed Aristotle, seeks to instantiate the good of its kind and will normally do so over time if not prevented by internal defect or external impediment. Hegel appropriated this concept and developed it carefully in his reflections on human nature. He also bequeathed it to Existentialism, the "human potential movement," and holistic psychologies of the twentieth century generally. Hegel's indirect—and sometimes direct—influence is apparent in all of these theoretical tendencies. Whereas Sigmund Freud's reflections were occupied with the neurotic, infantile, and unsuppressible side of the human psyche, those movements that stem from Hegel's work examine our capacity for autonomy and affirm our ability to grow into mature adults by projecting ourselves responsibly into the future.

To understand a bit better where this Hegelian emphasis has led, an example will help. Abraham Maslow (1908–1970) was an influential figure who was instrumental in refocusing professional psychologists' attention on studies of healthy human attainment. Writing more than a century after Hegel, Maslow put forward a "psychology of being" in which need-satisfaction terminates at the distinctively human level of self-actualization: "We share the need for food with all living things, the need for love with (perhaps) the higher apes, the need for self-actualization (at least through creativeness) with nobody."[5] Once humans reliably meet their basic needs, other needs develop in an ascending hierarchy. These needs represent more profound human strivings, and their fulfillment opens up correspondingly greater, more mature levels of contentment. Hegel could not have agreed more. In his terms, however, what is of most importance is that our species' special endowment—to comprehend the world thinkingly—comes to be actualized through a historical succession of attempts at locating the place of humans themselves within the scheme of things. And he enriches this story by overlaying it with a complex interpretation of the cosmic significance of the achievement.

Consciousness, for Hegel, emerges out of nature, and self-consciousness, out of mere consciousness. Then self-consciousness comes of age through arduous efforts aimed at refining its forms of comprehension. To secure an adequate understanding of this sequence of events is the primary purpose of Hegel's reflections on the human saga. But when self-conscious thought finishes digesting and retrospectively examining this process, he affirms, it accomplishes the very act of bringing the process to its completion. It thereby actualizes human knowing to the fullest extent. But simultaneously, a larger process is brought to fruition, which consciousness understands as the goal to which it has contributed. The internal dynamic of the activity thus described, then, is one of *consciousness understanding its progress through time, and its understanding signifies something of momentous importance.* Here we come into contact with the destiny of consciousness in a still broader sense.

Before we consider the larger significance of the journey consciousness undertakes, two clarifying remarks are in order. First of all, Hegel calls attention repeatedly to the capacity of thought to focus on its own processes. Critics of Hegel from his era to ours have often misconstrued this emphasis as a confession that he supposed thought to be concerned with idly rummaging through its own dusty attic or else with attempting to deduce truths about the world a priori. These contentions miss the mark. What Hegel intended was the following: (a) thought, in examining its own products, experiences a fluidity and freedom that push it ahead and beyond its own limitations (as we have seen in previous chapters); but also (b) in gradual stages, thought becomes explicitly what it had previously been only implicitly: the capacity to know reality adequately; and finally (c) thought is self-educating and self-disclosing. Thought is self-educating in that it is self-correcting and self-revising, with experience always as a vital reference point. Thought is self-disclosing as it reflexively sizes up its own powers. We see, therefore, that Hegel's doctrine of the reflexivity of thought is much more complex and of quite a different order from what his critics have alleged.

The second caution to be observed is that Hegel does not relegate human self-actualization to the arena of abstract thought alone. While he shares the age-old view that thinking raises humans to a level above that of animal life, there are many endeavors other than pure cognition that he esteems as contributing to the fulfillment of our human potential. Hegel's theory of human nature (which I discuss in chapter 6) may no doubt be faulted on numerous grounds, but narrowness of vision is not among them. Indeed, his concept of a well-rounded human being, as the spectrum of his works tells us quite transparently, also includes aesthetic, religious, social, ethical, political, intellectual, and historical dimensions.

One feature of the self-understanding of consciousness is its link with the actualization of human nature. But as I have hinted above, Hegel interprets this achievement in much wider, more dramatic terms. His account has two components. On the one hand, nature (the non-human physical world) also realizes its essence and fulfills its "destiny" by being known.[6] On the other hand, the Absolute (Absolute Spirit or God) manifests itself fully in and through human knowing. Common to both of these movements is that they are functions of self-realizing thought, and Hegel always presents them in this light. Accordingly, he affirms that as thought expresses its potential to know reality, by the same token nature manifests its "knowability," yielding up its secrets, so that the total structure of what *can* be known (the Absolute) shines forth.

THE GOAL OF KNOWLEDGE

Hegel again echoes Aristotle in positing that the intelligible essence of things is their formative aspect and is present in them. But for Hegel it requires a slow, painstaking process of inquiry for rational thought to unveil this truth and to reconcile itself with the world of things. In order to obtain such a result, everyday understanding, which abstracts and separates, must be supplanted by speculative reason, which perceives the universal in the particular and hence connects. What makes things be what they are is the ideal essence that is embedded in them, which Hegel calls a "concrete universal." That is, things physically instantiate the universal; it is literally *present and active in them*. By evolving an adequate comprehension of objects, one that penetrates to the core of their nature, then, we locate this indwelling "Concept" (capital "C"), liberating it to be known. And when we do this, we ultimately arrive at the point where there is no further antagonism between thought and things, where *the way things are thought to be or conceptualized is how they really are*. Hegel's students took this to mean that at this point, "the antithesis between subjective and objective (in its usual meaning) disappears."[7] (As Friedrich Nietzsche later wrote, "Coming to know means 'to place one-self in a conditional relation to something'; to feel oneself conditioned by something and oneself to condition it."[8]) Self and world, knower and known, thinker and world-thought-about are in harmony, closure is secured. This is not just because reflective thought has found the intelligible essence of things or worked out fully adequate concepts of them, but also, on a parallel track, because both consciousness and nature have actualized their potentialities within a relationship of interdependence.

As we see here, Hegel has "dialectically overcome" one of the most persistent and troublesome dichotomies of philosophical thinking— that of subject and object. Subject and object are normally assumed to be opposing and irreconcilable elements and to give rise to conflicting (subjective and objective) standpoints between which we are forced to choose. But, as Hegel argues, we do not have to choose because a more comprehensive and adequate perspective bridges the gap between these, or rather, shows that their separation was based on an erroneous, limited outlook of the understanding. Thought and things develop on parallel tracks: they interpenetrate; the "otherness" of each becomes subsumed, in turn, and they actualize each other's potentials. Indeed, our efforts to know have a certain destiny, as I have been saying, a career that is in harmony with the destiny of objects to be known:

> But the *goal* is as necessarily fixed for knowledge as the serial progression; it is the point where knowledge no longer needs to go beyond itself, where knowledge finds itself, where Notion [essential concept] corresponds to object and object to Notion. Hence the progress towards this goal is also unhalting, and short of it no satisfaction is to be found at any of the stations on the way.[9]

The pursuit of knowledge is a process that presses on, fueled by its inner dynamic and striving to coincide with, to reveal, the true nature of its object.

PANENTHEISM

We come at last to the supreme significance of the self-realization of consciousness (and indeed of nature, too). Hegel, here following the Jewish philosopher Baruch Spinoza (1632–1677), whom he greatly revered,[10] propounded the view known as *panentheism*, according to which God is both transcendent and immanent (to be contrasted with *pantheism*[11]). This entails that the Absolute is in some sense identical with both the *creative*, dynamic energy of nature and the cosmos but also with the sum total of what exists or has been *created*.[12] The Absolute is therefore in and of all things yet is not thereby spent as a force. Rather, the divine principle continues actively at work, flowing through nature and through time. As I indicated in chapter 2, Hegel is a process thinker, and the doctrine we are examining underlines the point. But his panentheism introduces the additional element that all rivulets of change and development manifest the presence of the Absolute, the infinite energy coursing through the finite realm.

Nature, then, is that which reveals the Absolute in the material realm. *Thinking* signifies the Absolute displaying itself in the medium of consciousness. Since these two are interlocked in a reciprocal relationship, their combined development represents the actualization or self-realization of the Absolute, or Absolute Spirit. It follows that in its final phases, the story of Absolute Spirit is coextensive with the story of Spirit (humanity) so that when Spirit actualizes *its* potentiality, it likewise actualizes the Absolute, which is working in and through Spirit. In other words, God's self-realization occurs through the vehicle of human self-realization. God is not a static entity that is perfect, complete, and self-contained for eternity; nor is God a detached occupant of a region "back of beyond." On the contrary, Hegel holds, God is in need of self-expression and modification through time and history, requiring particular circumstances through which to gain completeness (a concept to which we'll return in chapter 7). This is heady stuff, to be sure, and as I've noted, it constitutes a radical departure from orthodox Jewish, Christian, and Muslim theology. But while such ideas made Spinoza, for example, a lonely exile from the Jewish community of his native Amsterdam, Hegel stimulated the Romantic temper of his time, inspiring many to become Hegelians and process thinkers in the fields of philosophy and theology.

ADDITIONAL FEATURES OF ABSOLUTE SPIRIT

Hegel ventures still further into what some might regard as the dark night of wild and bizarre speculations. Yet given his basic method and outlook, we confront ideas that are entirely to be expected. Since the Absolute is immanently at work in nature and within human consciousness, the whole process of thought's reaching the highest truth is tantamount to God's "knowing himself" through humanity. Hegel identifies this level of knowledge as the attainment of "Spirit that knows itself as Spirit," or of "self-knowing reason."[13] He also refers, in this context, to "the self-thinking Idea, the truth aware of itself."[14] Less metaphorically, we might say that God's ultimate creative act is the one by means of which humans "bring it all together," acquiring the paradigm conceptual framework that exhibits the rationality of the cosmos. A simplified rendition of Hegel's extraordinarily complicated theory, as I have summarized it thus far, is contained in the diagram below.

As noted above (in chapter 3), Hegel contends that the Absolute, if it is to be discovered at all, must be present (or implicit in all of thought's

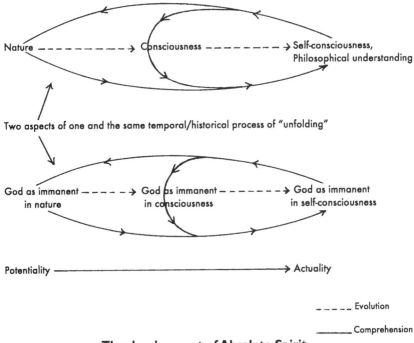

The development of Absolute Spirit.

dealings with the world) from the very beginning. The problem is that consciousness remains oblivious to this presence and only by a long and twisted dialectical route does thought win for itself the insight that it has all along been exploring the totality of things, but in various limited, inaccurate, merely perspectival ways. This is a theme to which Hegel returns over and over, expressing his desire to demonstrate that "the Absolute" is far from being a barren concept superimposed on our experience of, and reflection on, the world. Rather, it betokens the unifying tendency of rational thought that ultimately bursts forth to be acknowledged in its own right at the most advanced stage of philosophy. Furthermore, the Absolute is not an extramundane reality but is instead always at the heart of experience, immersed in the concrete details of life, including the dialectical skirmishes by which consciousness disentangles itself progressively from error and gains proper forms of comprehending.

One final facet of Hegel's treatment of the Absolute to be examined is its dialectical character. There are two aspects to this. In the first place, as I have noted, knowledge of the Absolute emerges gradually from the oppositional dynamics of thought in its self-revising and self-correcting movement. Inasmuch as thought seeks ever better conceptions that can pass the twin tests of experiential validation and critical inspection, the Absolute, as the progressively revealed subject of our efforts to understand the world thinkingly, may be said to comprise the increasingly broad and fertile contents of human mental life. Hegel complains that older kinds of "natural or rational theology" made God into a nebulous and remote entity, an "empty abstraction," which he deems to be "the dead product of the modern Enlightenment."[15] It is bad enough to posit a creator who is assigned the role of starting things off in the universe, establishing the laws of nature, and then retiring from the scene, as did the Deists of the eighteenth and nineteenth centuries (Voltaire, Jean-Jacques Rousseau, and Immanuel Kant, for example). Hegel scorned such thinking. Still worse, in his view, however, a God that is placed in a far-off, unreachable domain can have no clearly discernible qualities. It would follow that there could be no knowledge of God, since there would be nothing for cognition to lay hold of. Such an attenuated, distant God is anathema to Hegel. His concept of the Absolute, by contrast, is something that emerges in the dialectical struggle of knowledge, as it works its way toward the fullness of free self-expression. Successive attempts to comprehend reality, for Hegel, yield richer ideas of God, and these help liberate the human spirit to attain greater insight into the nature of things. Furthermore, the Absolute gains in complexity because it contains all of the negative elements or erroneous steps that characterize each stage of the crooked path by which it has been reached; for the truth, as we shall see in the next chapter, is the result plus the way that leads to it, the two being inseparable.

We have to really let all of this sink in if we want to appreciate what the Absolute means for Hegel. Many interpreters have been unable to do so or have lacked the patience. Bertrand Russell, for example, once charged that Hegel's Absolute is "a metaphysical showpiece[,] . . . an aloof and unknown entity wrapped up in its own thought."[16] However, coming to an appreciation of what Hegel had in mind should dispel such notions as products of external criticism that does not take the trouble or care to examine unusual ideas sympathetically and itself remains aloof to its subject matter. Russell, an otherwise extremely intelligent and acute thinker, allowed himself to succumb to this tendency. But Hegel clearly would have considered his own efforts futile if the Absolute were locked away in a distant sphere instead of being always present and operative in this world that we actually inhabit.

In the second place, the Absolute is dialectical in that, according to Hegel's script, God must externalize himself in creation in order to achieve self-realization. So far, this is not much different from more traditional theistic views to the effect that God's superabundance "overflows" or "emanates" and, in the process, brings entities into existence out of necessity. But Hegel, as usual, adds his own special twist to this position. He argues that God too must undergo self-estrangement by setting up an "other" in opposition to himself, then succeed in overcoming this alien phase of being in a higher act of self-recovery that signifies the attainment of wholeness and sufficiency, a victory over division and discontinuity. This "higher act," of course, is the comprehension of the entire process by human consciousness, which is, at the same time, the acting out of its final stages, in and through which the Absolute becomes actual by being fully known to, and by means of, finite human knowers, and also, thereby, to itself.[17]

WHAT "REVEALED RELIGION" REVEALS

In order to keep what is going on here in perspective, it is useful to realize that Hegel's theory attempts to resolve both epistemological and religious dilemmas. First of all, the universal is embedded in the particular, we have learned, and it is the contextualized or concrete universal we ultimately yearn to know. But our ordinary understanding cannot grasp this and forces us to choose between a perceived world that is a jumble of variegated particular things and an abstract realm of general laws, principles, and rules that are only reached by inference. As a community of knowers, we seek a coherent, harmonious outlook on experience that can reconcile these two perspectives. But we need greater conceptual maturity to assist us in reaching this goal—for example, some intelligible account that links observation to theory. Second, religiously speaking, God is typically characterized as "the supreme being," but "revealed religion" (by which Hegel means Christianity) features divine incarnation in human form, in the person of Jesus. Here again the universal (in this case, the Absolute being) is instantiated in the particular. But how can that which is transcendent be identical with what is merely human and mortal? Hegel (like other believers) simply says that this is the lesson of revealed religion. However, he comes at this teaching from an interesting angle. The "truth" of revealed religion is neither immediately nor adequately absorbed by human consciousness, which therefore remains alienated from this piece of knowledge. As often as the unity of divine and human, universal and particular, is represented in artistic images and prose, it still remains uncomprehended. But there is a Hegelian remedy. Each of us has to undergo identification with Jesus, personal sacrifice, and finally rebirth as a full-fledged member of the religious community in order to enact this unification.[18] Both of the areas of conflict reviewed here—epistemological and religious—can only be dissipated by the rational operations of metaphysical or "speculative" thought. It cannot be stressed too much that their resolution entails the cooperation and endorsement of a social community as well, in which the practice of faith and ritual are shared formative activities.

THE COSMIC DRAMA

Hegel's story of the Absolute may strike one as quite fanciful. It is difficult not to wonder what could possibly have motivated him to create it and what it really signifies. I have suggested in chapter 3 that no answer to these questions can be entirely satisfactory if the tale Hegel wishes to tell takes us back to a fundamental vision of his own. But to a degree we can understand what he is up to in terms of his project to fuse panentheistic Christianity with the ancient wisdom that *Logos* (or an immanent rational principle) governs the world. Joining these ingredients, as the above discussion elucidates, yields a powerful cosmic drama that Hegel wishes to persuade us is taking place all around us—and especially within and by means of us. This, I think, is the unique meaning he attaches to the outlook he is promoting. In the postmodern age, Hegel's metaphysics would be judged to embody a "metanarrative of legitimation," as I noted at the end of the last chapter. Postmodernists contend that we no longer find these credible, and for this reason it may be difficult for some readers to allow themselves to see the world as Hegel did. Many of his own contemporaries found his approach to be preposterous and beyond belief. Søren Kierkegaard, for instance, thought of Hegel's attempt to systematize existence within a religious outlook as "a venture in the comic."[19] But if one hopes to capture the pulse of Hegel's grand synthesis, such qualms will have to be put aside, if only temporarily, provisionally, and heuristically (in order to promote inquiry).

These remarks are in no way intended to serve as a caution against coming to a critical reckoning with Hegel, which is a task each reader must ultimately face. (I shall offer my own concluding assessment in chapter 7.) The important thing to keep in mind as we proceed, however, is that Hegel committed himself to sifting through an incredibly wide range of human experience and activity, looking for a unifying thread to make sense of it all. In addition, he is dedicated to the goal of rendering the changeable—the world of becoming—intelligible, rather than distorting it, either by ossifying it in concepts or by denying its reality and substituting an elusive sphere of being that lies on the far shores of experience. His metaphysical enterprise requires something like the consummate skills of a juggler, riding a unicycle on a tightrope, balancing an untold number of objects in a gravity-defying performance, whose craft is taken with the utmost seriousness. We can admire it even if part of us believes it can never be so perfect as to overcome all obstacles that stand in the way of a triumphant outcome. So it is with Hegel: We behold with awe the conceptual edifice he has built, but we can't be altogether sure whether we trust what he tells us about it. One consideration, internal to his own account, that may cause us to waver is this: If his philosophy did originate in a vision, as I believe, then in order to understand reality, something more is required than the purely rational view of the universe he so strongly favors. We would have to share his vision as well. And this is impossible, or at least improbable. Nonetheless, we are fascinated, and drawn in, by the power and degree of truthfulness we do find in Hegel. Even if one's final judgment on his work were to exhibit some degree of ambivalence, this would in no way detract from the value of one's encounter with it.

NOTES

1. Just to be clear, I wish to add that this has nothing to do with "spiritualism" of the sort that features the belief that a medium can bring the dead into contact with the living during a seance.

2. Charles A. Reich, *The Greening of America* (New York: Bantam Books, 1971), pp. 416–17. My thanks to Lenore Brashler for calling my attention to this passage.

3. W. H. Murdy, "Anthropocentrism: A Modern Version," *Science* 187 (1975): 1170.

4. We must remember that Hegel lived in a pre-ecological era, when the degree to which humans actually depend on nature was not so evident. Even now, there is a strong tendency to downplay or deny this fact, so it is hardly surprising that Hegel frames his theory in such terms. We may debate, and probably will continue indefinitely debating, the extent of our dependency on nature. However, Hegel certainly did not assume that we have none—indeed, quite the contrary, as we shall see in chapter 6.

5. A. H. Maslow, *Motivation and Personality* (New York: Harper and Brothers, 1954), p. 147. Maslow's theories are further amplified and refined in his later works *Toward a Psychology of Being*, rev. ed. (Princeton, NJ: Van Nostrand, 1968), and *The Farther Reaches of Human Nature* (New York: Viking Press, 1971).

6. We could say, paraphrasing Berkeley, that for consciousness *esse est intelligere* (i.e., its "to be" or essence is to understand) and for nature *esse est intelligi* (i.e., its "to be" or essence is to be understood).

7. G. W. F. Hegel, *Encyclopaedia Logic*, trans. T. F. Geraets, W. A. Suchting, and H. S. Harris (Indianapolis: Hackett, 1991), sec. 24, p. 56.

8. Friedrich Nietzsche, *The Will to Power*, trans. Walter Kaufmann and R. J. Hollingdale (New York: Random House, 1967), sec. 555, p. 301.

9. G. W. F. Hegel, introduction to *Phenomenology of Spirit*, trans. A. V. Miller (Oxford: Clarendon Press, 1977), sec. 80, p. 51 (emphasis in original). The allusion here to the stations of the cross is unmistakable.

10. "It is therefore worthy of note that thought must begin by placing itself

at the standpoint of Spinozism; to be a follower of Spinoza is the essential commencement of all Philosophy." See G. W. F. Hegel, *Lectures on the History of Philosophy*, trans. E. S. Haldane and Frances H. Simson, vol. 3 (London: Routledge and Kegan Paul; New York: Humanities Press, 1963), p. 257.

11. Pantheism is "the view that God is identical with everything. . . . Pantheism should be distinguished from *panentheism*, the view that God is in all things. Just as water might saturate a sponge and in that way be in the entire sponge, but not be identical with the sponge, God might be in everything without being identical with everything." See A. P. Martinich, "Pantheism," in *Cambridge Dictionary of Philosophy*, ed. Robert Audi, p. 640 (emphasis in original). Hegel rejects pantheism because he believes it reduces God to finitude. See G. W. F. Hegel, *Lectures on the Philosophy of Religion* (*One-Volume Edition: The Lectures of 1827*), ed. Peter C. Hodgson, trans. R. F. Brown, P. C. Hodgson, and J. M. Stewart, with the assistance of H. S. Harris (Berkeley: University of California Press, 1988), pp. 122–26, 260–63.

12. Spinoza's way of expressing this divine duality relies on expressions borrowed, as he acknowledges, from Scholastic philosophy: God is both *natura naturans* (literally "nature naturing") and *natura naturata* ("nature natured"). See Baruch Spinoza, *Ethics Demonstrated in Geometrical Order*, trans. W. H. White, in *Spinoza: Selections*, ed. John Wild (New York: Scribner's, 1958), Prop. XXIX, Scholium, p. 126.

13. Hegel, *Phenomenology*, trans. Miller, sec. 808, p. 493; G. W. F. Hegel, *Hegel's Philosophy of Mind*, part 3 of the *Encyclopaedia of the Philosophical Sciences*, trans. William Wallace and A. V. Miller (Oxford: Oxford University Press, 1971), sec. 577, p. 314.

14. Ibid., sec. 574, p. 313.

15. Hegel, *Encyclopaedia Logic*, sec. 36, p. 73.

16. Bertrand Russell, *Wisdom of the West* (London: Macdonald, 1959), p. 247.

17. The plausibility of this story has recently been defended by Edward Craig in *The Mind of God and the Works of Man* (Oxford: Clarendon Press, 1996).

18. I am grateful to Scott Meaney for suggesting this way of phrasing the issue.

19. Søren Kierkegaard, *Concluding Unscientific Postscript to Philosophical Fragments*, trans. Howard V. Hong and Edna H. Hong (Princeton, NJ: Princeton University Press, 1992), vol. 1, p. 34n.

5

TRUTH

TRUTH AND FALSITY

"Why bother with the false?" Hegel provocatively asks in his *Phenomenology of Spirit*.[1] The answer, as we have already gathered, is this: What we designate as true is that which evolves by means of a temporal process of trial and error, each stage of which contributes to the result arrived at in a way that is significant but not necessarily immediately apparent. In short, the outcome of his inquiries—or indeed of any inquiry—is unthinkable apart from the steps leading up to it, which are organically connected with it. The truth-finding process gives contextual meaning to the result we arrive at by integrating it into our knowledge-scheme. But in addition, when we reflect on the road we have traveled, the truth arrived at is seen to have vindicated its claim to acceptance. Hence, Hegel is quite scornful of the everyday view that posits truth and falsity as opposite extremes: "'True' and 'false' belong among those determinate notions which are held to be inert and wholly separate essences, one here and one there, each standing fixed and isolated from the other, with which it has nothing in common. Against this view it must be maintained that truth is not a minted coin that can be given and pocketed ready-made."[2] Truth, then, is not only the "kissing cousin" of falsity, it is something that must be won, a constant victory against odds. This concept is implicit in Hegel's perspective on the historical achievement of philosophy, which I laid out in chapter 1.

As usual, Hegel has something more in mind as well. This is that what is false (or what we might say has "negative epistemic value") plays a vital formative role in the production of the true (what has "positive epistemic value"):

> [T]ruth therefore includes the negative also, what would be called the false, if it could be regarded as something from which one might abstract. The evanescent itself must . . . be regarded as essential, not as something fixed, cut off from the True, and left lying who knows where outside it, any more than the True is to be regarded as something on the other side, positive and dead.[3]

Truth is like life: an ongoing development, characterized by passing phases of growth, which are themselves inseparable aspects of the moving current that constitutes its very being. We have here a dynamic and vivid image of truth as something that evolves, not just a dry result waiting to be recorded neutrally as a "fact," "state of affairs," or piece of "data."

TRUTH AS STRUGGLE

We must now enter further into Hegel's theory of truth because it is the glue that binds his system together. Hegel rejects the claim that a comprehensive metaphysical theory can be derived from basic assumptions or self-evident, supposedly axiomatic premises, as we have seen. In this important respect, he very clearly distances himself from the approach to philosophizing that was typical of Rationalists like René Descartes and Baruch Spinoza. So that there can be no doubt whatsoever as to where he stands on the issue, however, he states his own belief emphatically: "any so-called basic proposition or principle of philosophy, if true, is also false simply insofar as it is merely a basic proposition or principle."[4] The point here, perhaps somewhat abruptly asserted, is that any initial position in philosophy needs to be transformed, moved beyond. That being the case, we can only regard it as containing a provisional or partial truth, that is, *part of the truth* we seek and shall hopefully secure later on, but only after a painstaking journey of the intellect.

The idea that truth is attained by means of a long and arduous struggle and is literally the product of work (in this case, philosophical labor) has many progenitors, but it can be traced back most directly to Socrates.[5] For Socrates, dialectic (or philosophy), the process of interrogating and improving one's own understanding, is the practice that, engaged in with diligent effort, enables one to obtain the truth about things. Many of Plato's dialogues illustrate the point, but in *The Republic*, Socrates ventures still further, claiming that in the ideal educational system no one will be entrusted with the study of dialectic until the age of thirty—and even then, only after ten years of intensive mathematical training![6] We could plot the trajectory of this idea all the way down to works written by adherents of modern pragmatism, some of whom have held that truth is never more than an approximation to reality and others who stress that a true belief must somehow make a difference to the way we manipulate the world around us. Hegel's view, as we might expect, is distinctively different from any of these and more broadly conceived. For him, truth is the durable alloy that emerges from the fiery crucible of Spirit's self-critical quest for stability and rational order in its conception of the world. Yet, despite the important differences, there is also a strongly pragmatic element in his view, as we shall see. For remember that proper thinking entails testing results regularly against experience.

Philosophical inquiry is part of the self-education of humankind. Hegel, as we are aware, places it at the top of the list of truth-gathering activities because of its encompassing nature and complete dedication to the business of scrutinizing ideas and theories to determine their adequacy for capturing reality in its diverse, yet finally harmonious manifestations. But in keeping with his sense of the tragic aspect of life and world history, and of the dialectical quality of all knowledge attempts, the picture Hegel paints is not one of joyful levity. Rather, he highlights a task that is often burdensome, though not without its rewards, its consummation being "absolute knowing," as we saw in chapter 3. In a wonderfully evocative passage, Hegel expresses the insight that in matters of knowledge and creativity, just as much as in the social, political, and historical arena, we are our own worst enemies:

> Thus, the spirit is divided against itself; it has to overcome itself as a truly hostile obstacle to the realisation of its end. That development which, in the natural world, is a peaceful process of growth—for it retains its identity and remains self-contained in its expression—is in

the spiritual world at once a hard and unending conflict with itself. The will of the spirit is to fulfil its own concept [i.e. to realize its potential, its essential nature]; but at the same time, it obscures its own vision of the concept, and is proud and full of satisfaction in this state of self-alienation. Development, therefore, is not just a harmless and peaceful process of growth like that of organic life, but a hard and obstinate struggle with itself.[7]

One cannot overestimate the central importance of these remarks for consolidating our picture of Hegel's general position and theory of truth. It will be worthwhile, then, to spend some time in analyzing his words.

The first thing to note is that Hegel, in a manner both intriguing and engaging, has brought self-alienation to the forefront. What he is suggesting is that Spirit (here represented as the collective knowing consciousness of humanity) projects its formulations onto the world and then, for various reasons that ultimately originate within itself, finds them lacking. Initially, it confronts a hostile and surd barrier to its progress. Spirit, as Hegel personifies it, is hasty to locate the blame for this state of affairs in something outside itself: "Thus consciousness suffers this violence at its own hands: it spoils its own limited satisfaction. When consciousness feels this violence, its anxiety may well make it retreat from the truth, and strive to hold on to what it is in danger of losing. But it can find no peace."[8] For instance, consciousness sometimes posits myths or irrational hypotheses or simply makes incorrect judgments concerning how the world is. Other times it gets part of the story right but, undecided on where to turn next, casts about for alternatives and feels lost in a sea of choices or shrouded in mystery, and in either case undergoes the torment of uncertainty. These are translucent encounters with itself, with its own finitude and limitations, and as solutions, they inevitably prove futile.

Hegel's portrayal is especially interesting because he not only introduces the elements of striving and self-frustration into epistemology but also locates anguished yearning at its core. We can now understand better why Hegel says that Spirit "wins its truth only when, in utter dismemberment, it finds itself": the knowing process is like a house divided against itself, where healing, recovery, and wholeness must be found in the reconciliation of antagonistic factions and the overcoming of intransigence.[9] The context under discussion differs, however, in that consciousness has to rely on its *own* powers to disentangle the mess created by its blundering and more or less crude attempts at advancement. It must go through the phases of confronting "otherness, estrangement, and the overcoming of this estrangement."[10] Ultimately, consciousness must endure the chastening experience of its own humiliation and comeuppance in order to reach mature wisdom.

Every problem that confronts human ingenuity can provide an example, whether it is a project to survey the human genome, gain an understanding of the most basic constituents of matter, fathom the way ecosystems regulate themselves, divine the best approach to achieving equality of opportunity in society, or probe how we know anything by means of our sense organs. In each case, many wrong avenues have been pursued and many more revisions and adjustments introduced. What looks promising at first breaks down; consciousness finds itself in disarray and has to regroup for another try. When progress occurs, and most of all with ultimate success, there is some kind of closure in which human capacities receive validation (Spirit "finds itself," savors "reconciliation with itself," or "becomes at home in its other").

Hegel claims that the journey of the human Spirit toward enlightenment and self-betterment is quite unlike processes found in the non-human natural world. While it shares with living things the characteristic of organic development, the evolution of Spirit is unique. Hegel believes (rightly or wrongly) that a kind of monotonous repetition prevails in nature, where "development . . . retains its identity and remains self-contained in its expression," or, in other words, nothing spectacularly new or even especially noteworthy happens from one day to the next. In the restless domain of human achievement, by contrast, novel results are produced unrelentingly. There is always something new under the sun, rising from the detritus of the old by virtue of the constant dialectical activity of Spirit.

Finally, we are told that "The will of the spirit is to fulfil its own concept." Hegel means by this that Spirit is driven by its own inner momentum toward full self-expression, or self-actualization. That's the sort of dynamic entity it is. But at the same time, it does not clearly apprehend this goal and even dissimulates and does things that veil this objective from its own view. These behaviors prevent the attainment of its ends, which requires self-conscious and focused effort. Furthermore, Spirit is "proud and full of satisfaction in this state of self-alienation." The terrain that consciousness traverses is strewn with the litter of its own abortive and often disastrous products, disguised by self-deceptive maneuvers. (Recall the nonlinear path of dialectical progression pictured in chapter 3.) Hence, we can well appreciate why Hegel depicts our search for truth as "the path of doubt, or more properly a highway of despair."[11] He also tells us that consciousness has a certain haughty arrogance that sets it up for a fall. We often cling to the conviction of which Hegel speaks: that we are right, someone else is wrong; that we know everything so much better than did previous generations (or our children's); that our way is the best; that some immediately perceptible, facile solution is bound to be the correct one; and so on. Human consciousness displays its vanity, and many attempts to acquire knowledge ironically prove to be in vain as well. But this, it seems, is the hard lesson of life we are fated endlessly to relearn, and each of us, in his or her own years on the planet, reenacts many of the same dramas of knowledge-seeking that have already been played out by those who've gone before.

It is interesting and significant that Hegel's observations concerning the human Spirit divided against itself are reflected in many sayings from different lands and times. There is, first of all, this well-known slogan: "We have met the enemy and he is us," penned in 1970 by American cartoonist Walt Kelly and featured on an Earth Day poster the following year.[12] Many other noteworthy individuals, both before and after Hegel, have made similar statements as well. Here are some examples:

"What is man's chief enemy? Each man is his own."
(Anacharsis, sixth century BCE)[13]

"Formidable is that enemy that lies hid in a man's own breast."
(Publilius Syrus, first century BCE)[14]

"Man is wise . . . when he recognizes no greater enemy than himself."
(Marguerite of Navarre, 1558)[15]

"Our greatest foes, and whom we must chiefly combat, are within."
(Miguel de Cervantes, 1615)[16]

"[Y]et is every man his greatest enemy, and, as it were, his own executioner."
(Sir Thomas Browne, 1643)[17]

"Except Thyself may be
    Thine Enemy—
Captivity is Consciousness
    So's Liberty."

(Emily Dickinson, c. 1862)[18]

"It is hard to fight an enemy who has outposts in your head."
(Sally Kemptson, 1970)[19]

We find here that Hegel's insights once again resonate impressively with those of other creative and intuitive thinkers.

CLASSIFYING HEGEL'S THEORY OF TRUTH

How should we classify Hegel's theory of truth, which has so many singular and curious features? A common strategy is to place it within the context of the three main traditional views of truth: (a) the correspondence theory (truth is the resemblance between an idea and an object, a fact, or a state of affairs), (b) the pragmatic theory (truth is what "works," produces a desired result, makes a difference in the world, or issues in correct predictions), and (c) the coherence theory (truth is a relational property, a function of how well our beliefs are integrated, or "hang together," reinforce, or depend upon one another). According to this frame of reference, Hegel's notion of truth is generally thought to belong in category (c).

There is something to be said in favor of this interpretation, for Hegel does tell us more than once, "The true form in which truth exists can only be the scientific system of it," and, "The True is the whole."[20] Furthermore, we have seen that he regards the history of philosophy as a cumulative process leading to an overall result, which is an organized, integrated body of knowledge. It is tempting to conclude, therefore, that for him truth is a matter of coherence. At the same time, there are also some problems with this view. For one thing, critics frequently charge that the coherence theory is itself incoherent. This is owing to its apparent reliance upon the impossible fantasy of omniscience. The argument is that the theory generates the following reductio ad absurdum: If, in order to know anything at all, we must know everything, then we will never know anything, because it is obvious that we cannot know everything. Therefore, we cannot know anything—which is plainly false and indeed illogical, for to have reached this conclusion is to know *something* after all. But Hegel never says we must know everything in order to know anything. According to a well-known story, a self-important but minor philosopher named Wilhelm Krug once challenged Hegel to deduce the existence of his quill pen. The request was rightly dismissed as "naïve."[21] The point here is twofold: Hegel does not deduce his claims a priori (independently of experience), and he does not maintain that everything can be known. Hence, if his theory of truth may correctly be described as a coherence theory, this must be understood in a different sense than certain superficial stereotypes assume.

Another reservation about classifying his theory in this way concerns the fact that Hegel is much more of an empiricist than he is usually credited with being. As I have noted several times already, he defers to experience quite regularly in order to test his formulations.

Moreover, the three traditional theories of truth are arguably interdependent in that a well-defined account of truth implicates them all. It is fine for a set of beliefs about the world to have *coherence*, and indeed it ought to. But if that is all it has, it possesses no greater claim to our attention than other coherent belief sets, such as those composing pseudosciences like numerology and astrology, which also purport to apply to the world or to some significant portion of it. So, in addition to being coherent, a set of beliefs needs to correspond to the way things actually are (which also means they must "work," as the pragmatic theory holds). But beliefs that *correspond* must make sense too, which means they must "hang together," or cohere, and furthermore, they must be useful. Nor is this sufficient. It would certainly seem that any belief that displays *pragmatic* power, or "makes a difference" to what we do, must correspond to the way things really are in order to accomplish its purpose and must connect with the matrix or network of beliefs that governs our lives to be meaningful and fruitful. I argue that Hegel is aware of all these cross-references and takes them into account to a high degree. The sense in which coherence is a prominent feature of Hegelian truth should by now be evident. Hegel's attentiveness to experience confirms his commitment to the correspondence aspect of truth. And his doctrine that the truth may be metaphorically compared to the ontogenetic development of a fruit-bearing plant, from first bud to maturity (see chapter 2), illustrates his pragmatic leanings. So we must recognize that the nature of his project is to demonstrate—or more properly speaking, to allow thought spontaneously to show—the truth of the claim that "reality is rational" (which we shall examine in chapter 7). This conclusion, as Hegel develops it, then, illustrates all three aspects of truth that we have been examining.

The clue to unravelling Hegel's theory of truth is, in the end, however, to be found only when we ask what *kind* of truth he was after. It will aid our investigation to complete a quotation cited earlier only in part: "The True is the whole. But the whole is nothing other than the essence consummating itself through its development. Of the Absolute it must be said that it is essentially a *result*, that only in the *end* is it what it truly is; and that precisely in this consists its nature, viz. to be actual, subject, the spontaneous becoming of itself."[22] We pretty much know by now what Hegel means. The truth, considered holistically, is the process of its own genesis and growth and is not fully ripe until it is self-knowingly and self-critically apprehended as such. The truth is actualized when the self-conscious subjectivity of Spirit knows that the pathway it has traveled and the destination it has arrived at form a unitary movement that attains its (previously only implicit but now explicit) goal. Here we have one major part of his theory of truth.

Against this background, we can now digest the following passage, in which Hegel's students attempt to express the remaining part of his theory as he developed it in his lectures:

> In common life truth means the agreement of an object with our conception of it [i.e. correspondence]. We thus presuppose an object to which our conception must conform. In the philosophical sense of the word, on the other hand, truth may be described, in general abstract terms, as the agreement of a thought-content with itself. This meaning is quite different from the one given above. At the same time the deeper and philosophical meaning of truth can be partially traced even in the ordinary usage of language. Thus we speak of a true friend; by which we mean a friend whose manner of conduct accords with the notion of friendship. In the same way we speak of a true work of Art. Untrue in this sense means the same as bad or self-discordant.[23]

By "the agreement of a thought-content with itself," Hegel does *not* intend to designate ideas that have only the feature of coherence. (Indeed, coherence requires more than one belief or "thought," and more plausibly an entire network of beliefs, so this could not be his meaning.) What he has in mind, in contrast, is that it is when we reach the truth, thought comes to a resting point so that it no longer experiences internal discrepancies of the sort that propel it onward. The "disorderly conduct" of perspectives that are only partially true has been overcome by their subsumption in a more comprehensive view. The kind of idea thought then holds is "adequate to the content it expresses." This is the deeper sense of truth to which Hegel evidently alludes.

TRUTH AS SYSTEM

Now while we may be in possession of many small truths, such as those of mathematics, science, historical chronology, and ordinary experience, this is not what interests Hegel and emphatically is not what he refers to when he says that "the truth is the whole." If we adopt the standpoint that this phrase epitomizes, there is only *one* truth (or better: Truth, with a capital "T"). For only the systematic expression of the truth—that in which the dialectical flow of ideas is captured and rendered as a coherent, tightly interwoven web of concepts—is capable of revealing the full story about reality. In other words, an exhaustive, fully developed conceptual framework alone does justice to our experience, and we achieve satisfactory understanding of the world only within such a system.

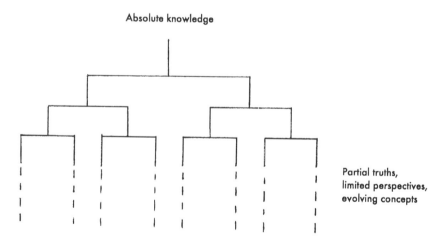

Absolute knowledge

Partial truths, limited perspectives, evolving concepts

The Truth is the entire system or network of results, increasingly rich in their interrelationships.

Individual entities are viewed in their proper perspective when apprehended as interrelated elements of an intelligible totality that has shown itself to correspond best to the way things really are. Notice, once again, that the entire process by which thought "comes to agreement with itself" can be described as one of *alienation* followed by *de-alienation*, in which it first discovers its own workings mirrored back to it by the world and appearing inadequate, then overcomes its "otherness" or deficiencies, and lastly "returns to itself" or becomes "at home with itself" as it perfects its performance.

Hegel's theory of truth plainly exhibits the essence of his thinking in general. Truth is something that emerges by means of a dialectical investigation, that makes explicit what it starts out as only implicitly, and that expresses itself as a self-actualizing totality, or *system*. "Truth," Hegel tells us, "is its own self-movement."[24] Such a notion has been warmly embraced by some but scathingly denounced by others. Søren Kierkegaard, for example, believed that systematic thought could neither embrace the richness of existence nor provide a foundation for the kind of resolute decision in favor of Christianity that he held a person of faith must make. Hegelian reasoning, he proclaimed, can never be more than "a method of approximation" to the highest truth.[25] Whether this criticism is really damaging to Hegel's project is, for now, best left to each reader to ponder. (I shall reconsider it in chapter 7.) But it should be made clear that what is at issue here is much more fundamental than may at first appear. Hegel did *not* boast that he could encompass all of existence in his system. A remark he makes in the *Philosophy of Right* illustrates his thinking on the matter: "To recognize reason as the rose in the cross of the present and thereby to delight in the present—this rational insight is the *reconciliation* with actuality which philosophy grants to those who have received the inner call *to comprehend*."[26] Here, Hegel tells us that the extent to which we perceive rationality in the course of events provides solace, even happiness and the determination to carry on. But he acknowledges, equally, that much of what confronts us in daily life is irrational and eludes our attempts to understand. Conflict, war, terrorism, treachery—these negativities are the bitter pills we must swallow along the difficult and vexed pathway to rationality in human affairs and to the universal realization of human potential. We need to remind ourselves that Hegel's goal was to disclose the intelligible structure of the world in general, not of everything that happens in it. Of course, Kierkegaard denied that it *has* such a structure—except, perhaps, for an all-knowing God. By his lights, Hegel believed he could take a God's-eye viewpoint and, in making this assumption, was sadly mistaken. Giving the last word to Hegel, however, it must be said that he did not conceive of what he was doing in this fashion; *it is God who thinks through us* and we who come to an awareness of actively participating in this process. Consequently, it is with God's aid that we discern the rational pattern underlying the chaos of everyday life and world events and thereby achieve some measure of inner peace, plus the determination to move forward.

TRUTH AND FALSITY REVISITED

Let us return now to the question with which this chapter opened: "Why bother with the false?" It is worth briefly juxtaposing to Hegel's view that of Friedrich Nietzsche, both because it bears an interesting resemblance to Hegel's and because it helps to crystallize Hegel's position for us. Nietzsche writes, "The falseness of a judgment is for us not necessarily an objection . . . ," and he exhorts his readers to "recognize untruth as a condition of life."[27] But Nietzsche is a *perspectivist*, one who asserts that all knowing is context-sensitive, meaning historically, culturally, and personally standpoint-dependent. Knowledge is relative to time and place, according to him, in a much more sweeping sense than it is for Hegel. No beliefs, for Nietzsche, have genuine objectivity or truth that is entirely independent of the mind. Hence, all that matters is how durable and practically beneficial (or "life-enhancing") they are: "Truth is the kind of error without which a certain species of life could not live," declares Nietzsche.[28] Both Hegel and Nietzsche agree that falseness does not necessarily constitute a fatal objection to a belief, and that truth, so far as it exists, needs to emerge slowly. But their reasons for supporting these positions are worlds apart. For Hegel, perhaps untruth is "a condition of life," yet this is a state of affairs that our species can transcend and that in some sense it is our destiny to transcend. "The truth will out," as they say. For Nietzsche, however, what we accept as truth is just the mask behind which the world hides itself from us. Here we have as divergent a pair of assessments as can be imagined. Nietzsche might have the greater number of followers today, but Hegel would say that Nietzsche is merely stuck in the same old relativistic epistemological rut from which Absolute Idealism promises to deliver us.[29]

The role that Hegel assigns to falsity must, then, be appreciated in its own terms. Occasionally, views such as his are illuminated by remarks that come from an unexpected source, from a voice that is speaking on behalf of a quite different knowledge-agenda. Here is a case in point. A distinguished American biochemist, reflecting on his research career, once observed: "By far the greater number of experiments scientists do are failures. We learn from our failures, and design better experiments that may eventually give us a new insight. . . . Most ideas are wrong, and one is very lucky to have a few good ones in a lifetime."[30] Hegel would doubtless be very pleased by these remarks. For his perspective that truth rises up from the ashes of the false could receive no stronger affirmation.

TRUTH TRIUMPHANT?

Hegel had a great deal of confidence in his own philosophy and in the readiness of the world to accept it. And he was not one to shy away from proclaiming his sense of the auspicious moment: "We must hold to the conviction that it is the nature of truth to prevail when its time has come, and that it appears only when this time has come, and therefore never appears prematurely, nor finds a public not ripe to receive it."[31] Elsewhere, he adds that "philosophy . . . is *its own time comprehended in thoughts*."[32] Again, what may look like pure conceitedness can be explained by reference to considerations that are internal to Hegel's system of ideas. In a sense, Hegel is simply the philosopher lucky enough to be able to articulate the result to which the dialectic of past philosophy has led, and that is now ready to emerge somewhere within the collective contemporary consciousness. There is a certain urgency or inevitability about this development, if we understand properly the steps that have led to it. And consequently, because the cultural group in which Hegel was temporally located constituted the collective consciousness of which *he* was a part, the stage was set for a receptive audience for his own philosophy.

We can appreciate where Hegel's position is coming from, and yet questions remain. There is the old maxim "The truth shall set you free," and often (even if not always) this is clearly so. Undoubtedly, the idea that truth liberates human possibilities is never far from Hegel's mind. But I think he was after something different. This is that the truth has a force of its own but needs fertile ground in which to take root. We must assume he is referring here to *philosophical* truth, for otherwise his statement is demonstrably false. For instance, Leonardo da Vinci proposed many inventions that were way ahead of their time, and world peace is an idea that today is far in advance of our readiness to accept or implement it. If, however, the human Spirit had evolved during Hegel's lifetime to the point where a view such as his could be formulated, then, given his theory of philosophy, it seems plausible that the time *was* ripe for its acceptance. But as the historical record shows, there are so many ideas of all kinds—including philosophical ones—that first appear and then must idly await acceptance for ages that Hegel's thesis becomes quite problematic. And as we shall see in the final chapter, Hegel's prognosis concerning the ripeness of the times for his own system proved correct—but only briefly. His philosophical claims to success were to be drowned out by the clamor of the "Young Hegelians" who followed him. Hegel's "truth" had a remarkably short "shelf life" and was then overthrown—the proverbial "fifteen minutes of fame" that pop artist Andy Warhol declared to be the fate of creative efforts generally. Meanwhile, subsequent developments in the world of ideas confirm that knowledge often evolves either too fast or too slow, and in too unpredictable a way, for Hegel's declaration to possess credibility.

NOTES

1. See Hegel's preface to *Phenomenology of Spirit*, in *Hegel: Texts and Commentary*, trans. Walter Kaufmann (Notre Dame, IN: University of Notre Dame Press, 1977), p. 414. See also G. W. F. Hegel, *Phenomenology of Spirit*, trans. A. V. Miller (Oxford: Clarendon Press, 1977), sec. 38, p. 22.

2. Hegel, preface to *Phenomenology*, trans. Miller, sec. 39, p. 22.

3. Ibid., sec. 47, p. 27.

4. See Hegel's preface to *Phenomenology of Spirit*, in *Hegel: Texts and Commentary*, trans. Kaufmann, p. 394, and Hegel, *Phenomenology of Spirit*, trans. Miller, sec. 24, p. 13.

5. *Hegel: Texts and Commentary*, trans. Kaufmann, p. 400, and Hegel, *Phenomenology of Spirit*, trans. Miller, sec. 27, p. 15. The theme of toil runs throughout this work.

6. Plato, *The Republic*, bk. 7, 535–41.

7. G. W. F. Hegel, *Lectures on the Philosophy of World History. Introduction: Reason in History*, trans. H. B. Nisbet (Cambridge: Cambridge University Press, 1975), pp. 126–27. Hereafter referred to as *Reason in History*.

8. Hegel, *Phenomenology*, trans. Miller, sec. 80, p. 51.

9. Ibid., preface, sec. 32, p. 19.

10. *Hegel: Texts and Commentary*, trans. Kaufmann, p. 390, and Hegel, *Phenomenology of Spirit*, trans. Miller, sec. 19, p. 10.

11. G. W. F. Hegel, introduction to *The Phenomenology of Mind*, trans. J. B. Baillie, 2nd rev. ed. (London: George Allen and Unwin; New York: Macmillan, 1949), p. 135. This corresponds to Hegel, *Phenomenology of Spirit*, trans. Miller, sec. 78, p. 49.

12. Walt Kelly (1913–1973), *Pogo* cartoon strip, 1970. Kelly published an earlier formulation in *The Pogo Papers*, 1953.

13. Anacharsis, Scythian philosopher (fl. c. 600 BCE), cited by Stobaeus, *Florilegium II* (fifth cent. CE), pt. ii, l. 43.

14. Publilius Syrus, Latin epigrammatist and compiler (fl. 43 BCE), *Sententiae*, no. 235.

15. Marguerite of Navarre (1492–1549), "Novel XXX, the Third Day," *The Heptameron, or Novels of the Queen of Navarre*.

16. Miguel de Cervantes (1547–1616), *Don Quixote*, pt. 2, bk. 5, chap. 8.

17. Sir Thomas Browne (1605–1682), *Religio Medici*, pt. 2, 4.

18. Emily Dickinson (1830–1886), *Complete Poems*, #384.

19. Sally Kemptson (1943?–), "Cutting Loose," *Esquire*, July 1970.

20. *Hegel: Texts and Commentary*, trans. Kaufmann, p. 372, and Hegel, *Phenomenology of Spirit*, trans. Miller, sec. 5, p. 3; Hegel, preface to *Phenomenology of Spirit*, trans. Miller, sec. 20, p. 11.

21. G. W. F. Hegel, *Hegel's Philosophy of Nature*, pt. 2 of the *Encyclopaedia of the Philosophical Sciences*, trans. A. V. Miller (Oxford: Oxford University Press, 1970), sec. 250, note to "Remark," p. 23. The philosopher Hegel refers to is Wilhelm Trangott Krug (1770–1842).

22. See above, note 21 (emphasis in original).

23. G. W. F. Hegel, *Hegel's Logic*, trans. William Wallace, 3rd ed. (Oxford: Clarendon Press, 1975), sec. 24, p. 41.

24. Hegel, preface to *Phenomenology of Spirit*, trans. Miller, sec. 48, p. 28.

25. Søren Kierkegaard, *Concluding Unscientific Postscript to Philosophical Fragments*, trans. Howard V. Hong and Edna H. Hong (Princeton, NJ: Princeton University Press, 1992), p. 37.

26. G. W. F. Hegel, preface to *Elements of the Philosophy of Right*, ed. Allen W. Wood, trans. H. B. Nisbet (Cambridge: Cambridge University Press, 1991), p. 22 (emphases in original). Hegel uses this same image in his *Lectures on the Philosophy of Religion*, ed. E. B. Speirs, trans. E. B. Speirs and J. Burdon Sanderson, vol. 1 (London: Routledge and Kegan Paul, 1962), pp. 284–85.

27. Friedrich Nietzsche, *Beyond Good and Evil*, trans. Walter Kaufmann (New York: Vintage, 1966), sec. 4, pp. 11, 12.

28. Friedrich Nietzsche, *The Will to Power*, trans. Walter Kaufmann and R. J. Hollingdale (New York: Random House, 1967), sec. 493, p. 272.

29. As my former philosophy professor and mentor, Emil L. Fackenheim, used to exclaim, "Hegel refuted Nietzsche (or some other thinker) before he was born!"

30. Mahlon B. Hoagland, *The Roots of Life* (New York: Avon, 1979), pp. 111, 118.

31. Hegel, *Phenomenology of Spirit*, trans. Miller, sec. 71, p. 44.

32. Hegel, preface to *Elements of the Philosophy of Right*, p. 21 (emphasis in original).

6

ON BEING HUMAN

INTRODUCTION: FACETS OF THE SELF

A great deal of Hegel's energy is devoted, as we have seen, to elaborating his vision of reality as a rationally intelligible, dynamically developing whole made up of disparate but interconnected and complementary parts. We have examined this conception from various angles, and it is time now to consider how individual human lives fit into the picture. Hegel has insights into the human condition that are both challenging and important and that have left a fertile legacy to social and political thought. An acquaintance with these will be good preparation for encountering Hegel's writings that concern the shape of human life, as many of them do. In this chapter the emphasis will be on the self as a social construct and on the individual within the context of the state and world history. I will consider in some detail three of Hegel's most influential texts: (1) the section on "Independence and Dependence of Self-Consciousness: Lordship and Bondage" (*Phenomenology of Spirit*, B, IV, A), (2) the *Philosophy of Right*, and (3) *Reason in History* (the introduction to *Lectures on the Philosophy of World History*).

Hegel's *Phenomenology of Spirit* is a rich, multilayered work of great difficulty that requires patience to absorb but that also yields rewards in equal measure. It can be read in several ways, much as a major novel, such as *Don Quixote*, *Moby-Dick*, or *Ulysses*, can be read. One important approach to the *Phenomenology* sees it as the story of human consciousness traveling from naive innocence and bogus self-sufficiency to the sophistication of a critical, all-embracing world outlook attained through its own efforts. A variation on this theme portrays the work as a record of human self-discovery, in which the self—viewed both individually and collectively—creates itself and realizes its potential as both knower and doer. There is a spiritual aspect to this as well, and Hegel suggests we view the work as "the way of the Soul which journeys through the series of its own configurations . . . so that it may purify itself for the life of the Spirit."[1] Within the framework of this interpretation, the dialectic of "lordship and bondage" (rendered alternatively by different translators as "master and slave," "master and servant," "masterdom and slavery," "lord and bondsman") occupies a special place.

In this section of the *Phenomenology*, Hegel establishes three main points: (a) that being a self entails activity (a self is an affirmative force in the world), (b) that a self is what it makes itself to be through its own labor (a self is what it does), and (c) that the creative process in which selves arise is one of mutual recognition (a self comes to be born and to know itself through the mirror of social interaction). All of these are extremely important claims, and all have been enormously influential. Let us see how Hegel develops his theory.

To begin with, the idea that a self is what it does has a distinctly modern, existential ring to it. Jean-Paul Sartre, for example (in his earlier writings), is well known for defining a self or person as one who makes himself or herself emerge out of "nothingness" at each instant, one who is constantly projecting into the future, that is, choosing what he or she shall be. In contrast to this "process" view, there is a lengthy tradition in Western philosophy, of which René Descartes is the exemplar, according to which the self or person is a fixed thing, substance, or permanent and unchanging core of some kind that underlies and unifies one's experience. But in order to situate Hegel properly, we must appreciate that these theories are not the only players on the field. Partially in reaction to the Cartesian view, David Hume (1711–1776) notoriously proposed that the self is "nothing but a bundle or collection of different perceptions, which succeed each other with an inconceivable rapidity, and are in a perpetual flux and movement."[2] Another equally influential and controversial standpoint derives from Hinduism and Buddhism and states that the self is ultimately an illusion of our limited perspective on reality (the "no-self" view). Perhaps it is like an onion, whose layers we peel away, only to find a vacant center, or per-

haps it is just an assemblage of roles we play. Western authors like Her-
mann Hesse and Luigi Pirandello have explored such possibilities
relentlessly in their fictional creations. More recently, additional perspectives have come to the fore. One features the self as a relational
entity, a function of all the persons, places, and things in one's experience. The "expanded self" of the "deep ecology" movement is an entity
of this kind. The self as a purely social product—the "structuralist
self"—is characteristic of another modern movement of thought, struc-
turalism. An additional contemporary approach styles the self as a narrative (or group of narratives) constantly open to revision; this is one
version of the "postmodern self."

Hegel's theory is best identified with the idea that the self is an
active, self-making agent, and to this extent he is the progenitor of existentialism.[3] But Hegel's self is also a mutual project, something that
only arises within a social community of like beings. This is because
reciprocal recognition and affirmation are conditions he thinks are
required for fully developed selfhood.[4] Interestingly, empirical evidence
backs up this Hegelian claim. Studies of feral children (those adopted
and reared by wild animals), rare and anecdotal though they are, indicate that humans who are deprived of contact with members of their
own species fail to develop crucial language and social skills. Trans-
ferred to human society, these unfortunates fare poorly and die young.[5]
Furthermore, Leo Buscaglia, a professor of education and an expert and
popular speaker on the subject of love, cites several studies in one of his
books that suggest "a positive correlation between human concern and
togetherness, and human growth and development," arguing that a lack
of love can precipitate illness and "even bring on [a person's] death."[6]
Harry F. Harlow's cruel social isolation experiments, performed on
infant monkeys from the 1950s to the '70s, also confirm the need for
attachment in normal psychological development.[7] These points are
worth remembering as we work our way through Hegel's more philosophical treatment of the topic of selfhood. Like many of the greatest
philosophers, Hegel adopts a mode of analysis that is both conceptual
and enriched by psychological insight. As he affirms, "*Self-consciousness
achieves its satisfaction only in another self-consciousness.* . . . A self-consciousness exists *for a self-consciousness.* Only so is it in fact self-consciousness; for only in this way does the unity of itself in its otherness
become explicit for it. . . . [as] 'I' that is 'We' and 'We' that is 'I'."[8] This
seems paradoxical, for how can two self-consciousnesses recognize each

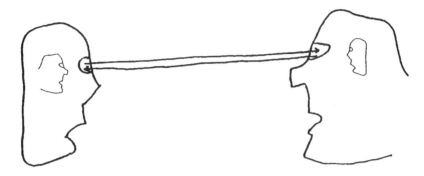

Self-recognition through the Other.

other unless they *already* exist as such? Clearly, something complex and elusive is being posited here. Why he says these things will now be investigated.

MASTER AND SERVANT: RECOGNITION AND SELFHOOD

Hegel represents the quest for selfhood in the metaphorical guise of a struggle for survival. To begin with, having traced the career of consciousness as a knowing capacity through the first lengthy part of the *Phenomenology of Spirit,* he introduces desire (or appetite) as the ingredient responsible for switching on our specifically human engagement with the world of objects. In humans, desire is not mere wanting; it is the will both to actively fashion what is external and to assimilate or otherwise appropriate this "other." Desire also affirms that we are *embodied* consciousnesses, who are *in* and *of* the world; we are anchored there. (As Martin Heidegger [1889–1976] would later assert, human being is *Dasein,* literally "there-being," or a kind of existence that discovers itself already situated or "thrown" into a natural and social environment.)[9] Moreover, desire, as Hegel speaks of it, contains the energetic impulse to selfhood in its latent, as yet undeveloped form. In Hegel's scenario, two desiring preselves encounter each other. Each strives to dominate its rival, doing violence if necessary to achieve this aim. But a mortal finish will not advance the cause of selfhood because recognition by the other is a crucial ingredient of one's identity. A lifeless other will not be able to provide the feedback needed to spur self-development onward. Therefore, Hegel posits an outcome of his hypothetical struggle in which one party either becomes subdued by, or submits to, the opposing counterpart. We come here to the famous master/slave relationship that has been appropriated and transformed by so many other writers since his time.

Before proceeding to examine this phenomenon, however, it is worth observing that Hegel's account should not be construed merely as a variation on the tired old theme of the state of nature as a condition in which mutual hostility reigns. Rather, he has a much richer topic in mind, namely, the many levels on which human beings struggle for their birth, identity, and integrity as individuals and for self-assertion and supremacy. From the earliest stages of life, we each seek ("desire") to affirm our independence, bucking against the constraints that limit us. In the first instance, we are bent on survival and the satisfaction of basic needs. As infants, we are very needy; one might even say that we are "pure need." Such "selves" as we are consist of primal impulses and the ability to manipulate those who serve us. As children, and later as adolescents, we carry the same bundle of needs forward, but we also become more assertive and strain against the limits our parents set for us. Still later, as adults, we jockey for position in social situations, on ladders of success, in romantic relationships, and in many other circumstances. Somewhere along the way we also develop the capacity for self-criticism, becoming able to judge ourselves, sometimes even "doing battle with ourselves." What is common to all these stages is the impetus of self-expression, the surging up of the self in confrontation with adversity. That we not only struggle against others but also internally against ourselves should be no surprise if we recall Hegel's wise insight that the dialectical nature of consciousness makes it its own worst enemy, always creating obstacles to its own progress (see chapters 2 and 5).

As in life, so it is with Hegel's imaginary preselves in conflict: some resolution of their yearnings will eventuate, but inasmuch as each side seeks unrestricted self-expression, the resolution embodies instability and tension. This restless element provides the momentum that drives the dialectic of selfhood onward, as we shall see. The first resolution, already noted, is the master/slave relationship, in which the master achieves a style of selfhood that is based on denial (negation) of the slave's selfhood. The slave is the vehicle or instrument of the master's will and experiences his or her life as being merely the means to another's ends. There are, of course, many examples of this unfortunate set of dynamics in what we like to call "real life": marriages in which husbands dominate and oppress wives, families with domineering mothers, ruthless dictatorships, situations of ethnic or religious persecution, child abuse, exploitative labor (actual slavery and "sweat shops"), sexual exploitation, and just the more ordinary kinds of psychological manipulation that go on in defective or diseased personal and professional relationships. I think, however, that Hegel would say even "normal" relationships (including, as above, one's relationship to oneself) feature ongoing struggles for ascendancy and recognition at many levels. Nor are these necessarily fixed and one-sided: sometimes one party dominates, sometimes the other. For instance, even in an ongoing, healthy sexual relationship, one lover may take the active role, the other the submissive role; on another occasion these roles may be reversed. And there are times when children act more like grownups, while their parents behave more like children.

Hegel's deep understanding of human nature makes itself evident in his awareness that the master/slave or dominance/submission relationship is not only unstable but also premised on modes of false consciousness. In Hegel's prototypical confrontation, the master's selfhood, as already pointed out, amounts to little more than the negation of another's desire for selfhood. The slave's existence, on the other hand, assumes the inertness of instrumentality and embodies self-denial. Furthermore, the slave undertakes the task of working on behalf of the master, "mediating," through physical labor, between nature and the master. (Nature likewise is the mediating element between the slave and the master, and the master mediates between nature and the slave because it is via the master's orders and intimidations that the slave works "for his or her life.") The master delegates to the slave the activity of satisfying his or her basic human needs while "living the life of luxury" and is thereby once removed from contact with the world. But in this configuration, the master becomes alienated from the very source of doing from which all selves derive (the self is a doer and is what it does; the master becomes a nondoer). The slave, then, is oddly enough a step closer to realizing full selfhood—as a being who is also a doer— than is the master. The master, by treating the slave as a mere thing or means, also denies to himself or herself the sort of mutual recognition needed for fuller forms of selfhood.

When it slowly begins to dawn on the slave that it is *because of slave*

labor that the master's identity is sustained, this is an empowering realization. The slave comes to learn that rebellion ("negation of the negation"—that is, confronting the master's negatively constructed selfhood) can help to overthrow an oppressive condition of existence and
that altering the dynamics of the master/slave relationship in this
manner knocks away the props that support the master's masterhood.[10]
In a simultaneous development, the master comes to an awareness that
his or her own "masterly" self is in truth one of dependence: One can
be and remain a master only so long as one's servants persist in their
craven submissiveness. Master and slave, then, are locked in a relationship that is both symbiotic and parasitic. To be a master is not an
achievement but rather a negation or deprivation of the other's freedom
to be a self, but by the same token, this also means that the master's life
is controlled by, and is a product of, the role that the slave takes on. So
similarly in everyday life many self-images are constituted by, and thrive
upon, putting others down, deceitful manipulation, intimidation, bul-
lying, gamesmanship, pulling rank, and so forth. These modes of being
a self are sustained by the acquiescence of others who are submissive
and whose potential for rebellion makes the dominant person's position always precarious and vulnerable to change.[11]

The slave, of course, has been little more than a dependent being, a
subhuman supplicant, whose very existence continues at the master's
pleasure and whim. Yet Hegel believes an important dynamic element
is present in the slave's consciousness of self, such as it is, that is missing
from the master's. This is that the slave remains in intimate contact with
the natural world and, through physical work, transforms it. This transformation is a very concrete avenue to self-discovery, for by means of it,
the slave is enabled to gain a sense of agency by having a personal
impact on the environment and by experiencing the fruits of his or her
own labor. Here again, Hegel shows himself to be anything but an
abstract and aloof thinker. On the contrary, he displays a commitment
to the proposition that it is only when human beings preserve and nur-
ture an active connection with the natural world that they grow,
develop, and attain well-being.

These early steps to selfhood that I have been discussing are outlined on page 126.

Phase I

Master
dominator
consumer
independent
firm self-image (pride, control)
inactive vis-à-vis nature (leisure)

Servant
dominated
producer
dependent
frail self-image (fear, service)
active vis-à-vis nature (labor)

Phase II

Master
mere negation (of servant's will
  and independent selfhood)

no further self-development
  (in this role)

Servant
creative negation
  (transformation of nature,
  to serve needs of other)
gradual self-development
  (in spite of this role)

Phase III

Master
selfhood unstable, based on
  illusions of supremacy
dawning experience of dependence

Servant
freedom emerging

first sense of potential
  independence

The dialectic of master and servant.

This summary, of course, represents only part of the tale because, as we have already gathered, the slave's (or former slave's) incipient selfhood is thus far grounded in negation in equal measure with that of the former master. The slave has not yet begun to become a mature self but has only alleviated the exploitative situation somewhat. Therefore, many further steps or dialectical developments have to be run through before fully adequate selfhood is secured by either party. The master has made a contribution by being a risk taker; the slave, by being the one who submits, has a spark of rebellion within and first comes to an awareness of the mutual dependency of selves. These inputs are filtered by the ongoing dialectical process of human growth and refined into new stages of selfhood.

But what we have learned about human life so far is of crucial importance. Through the active transformation of labor and consumption, the natural needs of the individual are met. Selfhood is a reciprocal project in which nature is the primary mediating factor. By means of engagements with other humans in our physical environment, we come to achieve personal affirmation and a sense of belonging. The master/slave dialectic reinforces the lesson that "every shape of consciousness has a future and a past."[12] That is, its origin and destination are both formative elements of what consciousness is at any moment in time. And last, all human relationships are political, involving the elements of power struggle, compromise, and, ultimately, negotiated resolution.

THE POLITICAL AND ETHICAL SELF

We need not trace all the intricate byways along which the self conducts its journey to fulfillment or actualization for Hegel. Suffice it to say that the concept has been established that selfhood requires a social context in which to play out its potentialities. But in order for selves to flourish, the form of this interaction must be one that is respectful, cooperative, and mutually validating. At first a dim, barely conscious awareness, the process here sketched comes into full bloom as the *Phenomenology of Spirit* unfolds. The details of Hegel's exposition concern how this perspective emerges as ever more apparent. His ultimate goal is to demonstrate that the highest level of self-actualization occurs in political society, indeed within the state. Why is this? The short answer is that it is this institutional framework that makes available to each person the maximum degree of independence and self-expression consistent with mature forms of reciprocal recognition.

An individual's search for selfhood is a development in which his or her independence is paramount. But as we know, for Hegel independence is also dependence in equal measure. We think and talk a great deal about freedom and value it supremely. Hegel did likewise. For him freedom is the condition of independent selfhood, or rather independence within, and because of, a network of dependence relationships. It is therefore a dialectical construct. Freedom must be contrasted with license, as many have acknowledged. *License* we may characterize as unrestricted freedom, or freedom that is amorphous, anarchic, directionless, and therefore ineffectual. *Freedom*, on the other hand, is focused liberty that exists within a structure of rights, privileges, rules, expectations, trust, and cooperation—in short, within an ethical and political community. Hegel's firm belief was that this structure is best provided by a state, or rather *is* a state, whose laws define the legitimate and illegitimate expressions of freedom. Laws, for him, are not abstract or arbitrary prescriptions, imposed by some remote authority as constraints that merely encumber people's lives and stifle individuality. On the contrary, they are the preeminent manifestation of people's wills, the true expression of freedom directed toward its own necessary self-restraint and rational guidance. Each of us is "present in the laws" so to speak; we are "externalized" in them, and they "internalize" all of our separate wills. They issue (ideally at least) from our collective freedom, from our acts of citizenship by means of which we creatively affirm and mold our independent selves in a spirit of togetherness, and we identify with them because of this. As we sometimes hear it said today, our individual wills are "invested" in the laws by which we've agreed to live. But the wills to which Hegel refers are rational wills, not merely desiring or feeling wills, and this is why their joint investment in the laws gives them the force of authority. This authority is not one of imposition but instead stems from the voluntary collaboration of self-aware participants in the political order.

So that we can gain a better appreciation of what Hegel is getting at, and the manner in which he makes his case, a consideration of his line of argument in the *Philosophy of Right* will be helpful. In this work, Hegel aims to portray the development of the individual through and by means of the various dimensions of social and political life in which he or she participates. These dimensions, in turn, express or manifest the individual's will in different guises, and each guise contributes to the realization of a rational order in human affairs. The rational order one's will helps to build is ultimately the actualization of Spirit as such in (1) the interactions of citizens, (2) the institutions they have created in order to facilitate such interactions, and (3) the form of ethical life that provides the framework for both (1) and (2). It is endemic to Hegel's thought that social and political ways of organizing human life are driven at a deep level by the quest for freedom that is pervasive, albeit often concealed from view. The *Philosophy of Right* discloses this crucial tendency and the dialectical path by which freedom comes to

maturity. In the relatively modern vision of the state toward which
Hegel's discussion leads, historically earlier types of alienation that prevented the cementing of social bonds, the progressive evolution of community, and a political sense of belonging are said to be finally overcome. Also, as is typical of Hegel's procedure, how the *Philosophy of
Right* unfolds is determined in part by the development of his own
ideas and in part by his strategy of demonstrating the limitations of
other approaches to the topic at hand.

The individual self is first presented in the *Philosophy of Right* within
the sphere of "abstract right" (sections 34–104). The focus here is on
persons exercising arbitrary free choice, engaging their wills with the
world of material things as insular and atomistic egos. They are characterized at this stage as possessors of property and of certain rights (such
as the rights to life, liberty, property, and happiness asserted by the "natural rights" tradition), as parties to contracts, and as subjects of laws
concerning torts and crimes, with the appropriate punishments at-
tached thereto. Hegel argues that from this standpoint, we are seen just
as creatures of self-interest who have an instrumental relationship with
our natural and artifactual environments and who stand in a formal
relationship with other human beings—such as we might label, somewhat neutrally, as "respecting their rights." (Contracts, for example, are
merely contingent agreements meant to insure that people's private
interests are united for a limited time and purpose and nothing more.)
While this cold and somewhat perfunctory way of viewing the self is
important and discloses much of the institutional framework in which
our lives and aims are consolidated and secured, there is much more to
being human. And in showing this, Hegel attempts to chart a larger
domain of selfhood, personal freedom, and community than those
provided by classical versions of social contract theory and liberalism.

We next witness the self embedded in the context of "morality"
(*Moralität*), wherein the subjective "immediacy" examined in the
domain of abstract right begins to become shaped by a richer understanding of what it is to be a responsible agent. Purpose, intention, con-
scientiousness, and pursuit of the good are the kinds of factors that
make us moral beings, Hegel avers, but it is to be noted that we are still
looking at behavior set apart from the complex social milieu in which
self-realization is really achieved. The main lesson Hegel teaches in this
part of the *Philosophy of Right* (sections 105–41) seems to be that neither
the private and strong deliverances of conscience nor the empty Kantian

formula of "duty for duty's sake" can fully capture what it means to be a rational free agent (and hence, as well, what it means to be an autonomous moral subject and a citizen). For this, we need to push further, into a more encompassing sphere in which the diverse elements of agency can be unified. As he puts it, "the identity—which is accordingly *concrete*—of the good and the subjective will, the truth of them both, is *ethical life*."[13] There is something of general significance in the conception and pursuit of the good, but also an important contribution to motivation is made by the particularity of the individual will. The interweaving of these two aspects is the ethical life, which represents both the universal and the singular combined into a new unity, Hegel calls "concrete," in order to demarcate it as an objective and meaningful way (or set of ways) of being in the world.

The final and lengthiest part of the *Philosophy of Right* (sections 142–360) is devoted to an account of the "ethical life" (*Sittlichkeit*), which situates morality (in the broader sense we usually give it rather than in the narrower sense considered by Hegel in the previous part on *Moralität*) as a definitive *social and communal* phenomenon. It is here that we acquire a familiarity with our roles as members of a family, of civil society, and of the state. In the ethical life, personal freedom finally loses its anarchic edge as it redirects itself from purely private projects to those that seek the overall good, the universal ends of humanity that we need to work together in order to obtain. What Hegel delineates here is that sense of common purpose on which cultures and political orders as we conceive of them today are based and from which they derive their character, ethical legitimacy, strength, and resiliency. It is as individual, free, rational subjects, not merely as self-seeking subscribers to a social contract, that we take our places in the objective world and respond to the practical demands that arise from our positions within it. Only such beings have the capacity to recognize ethical ends as worthy of advancing by means of their individual actions and commitments. (Hegel observes that "it is only as *thinking* intelligence that the will is truly itself and free."[14]) This is where the idea of something's being "for the good of us all" acquires genuine and durable content rather than merely being notionally conceded. Separate, but nonetheless dependent, selves can engage in joint ventures of fulfillment and social betterment within the enabling sphere of the ethical life. As many commentators have remarked, Hegel harks back here to the ancient Greek polis, which in its most perfected form, notes Charles Taylor, was a model to behold. Taylor writes: "The happiest, unalienated life for man, which the Greeks enjoyed, is where the norms and ends expressed in the public life of a society are the most important ones by which its members define their identity as human beings. For then the institutional matrix in which they cannot help living is not felt to be foreign. Rather it is the essence, the 'substance' of the self."[15] For Hegel the task was to recover this harmonious sense of belonging in a modern, more universally participatory, and rational setting.

The family is the locus in which an individual first learns of his or her identity with the universal through the closeness of association made possible by marriage (itself a transforming union of separate persons) and the effects of love (described by Hegel as "spirit's *feeling* of its own unity").[16] But the family is not a static entity or a final resting place. Individuals go forth from it to seek their fortunes, their self-affirmations in the world. The arena of relationships now entered is that of civil society, a realm of economic activity in which the particularity of each is reasserted but within a nexus of institutions that provide some features of universality: Hegel speaks of civil society as comprising "the system of needs," including the specialization of labor and the different classes or estates that grow up around these (sections 189–208), the system of justice that protects property (sections 209–29), police, and corporations (sections 230–56). This rather diverse assemblage yields Hegel's portrait of the dynamic structure of capitalist society.

THE STATE: WHERE SELFHOOD FLOURISHES

In concluding his perusal of the above elements of the ethical life, Hegel declares, "The sphere of civil society thus passes over into the *state*."[17] By this he means to signal a dialectical transition, but what is it that creates the need for one? The answer is given in sections 257–329 of the next (and last) subdivision of the *Philosophy of Right*, namely, that the state is the sine qua non of both the family and civil society. In other words, the family and civil society were dealt with first in order to show that, vital though they are to human life, both are incomplete and inadequate expressions of ethical life when considered apart from the state. Indeed, there is no ethical life, in Hegel's opinion, outside of the organic body of the state. "In actuality, therefore," he asserts, "the *state* in general is in fact the *primary* factor; only within the state does the family first develop into civil society, and it is the idea of the state itself which divides into these two moments."[18] More simply, he adds: "The state is the actuality of the ethical Idea—the ethical spirit as substantial will, *manifest* and clear to itself, which thinks and knows itself and implements what it knows in so far as it knows it."[19] In brief, the state is that reality within which the true, most complete ethical identity of the populace is articulated and instantiated by the actions of each and all. These actions are self-conscious to whatever degree we have achieved an understanding of our place in the overall process. The state, then, is not something over and above the communal life we share; it *is* just that life in its fullest manifestation.

As unifying communities, both the family and civil society already contain features of the state, but in nascent form. This is especially so in relation to civil society. Many writers before and after Hegel treated what he calls civil society as equivalent to the state, but Hegel insists on differentiating them quite clearly.[20] As a dialectical thinker, however, he sees the latter as "the truth" of the former, that is, the state configures the larger sphere in which the impulse and energy of civil society gain rational intelligibility and purpose and in which civil society has its internal contradictions reconciled. Civil society, says Hegel, may be thought of as "the *external state*," by which he means that the ingredients of a supervening wholeness are present in it but are not yet fully actualized.[21] However, a much more powerful point needs to be made, and this is that as individual selves, we must be members of a state in order to achieve validation as free, rational agents because it is only within the state that competing interests are fairly balanced. The explanation of this is that the state provides a comprehensive framework of governance and institutions that support ethical life and succeed in melding the individual and universal elements of humanity. Hegel elaborates:

> If the state is confused with civil society, and its determination is equated with the security and protection of property and personal freedom, *the interest of individuals as such* becomes the ultimate end for which they are united; it also follows from this that membership of the state is an optional matter.—But the relationship of the state to the individual is of quite a different kind. Since the state is objective spirit, it is only through being a member of the state that the individual himself has objectivity, truth, and ethical life. *Union* as such is itself the true content and end, and the destiny of individuals is to lead a universal life; their further particular satisfaction, activity, and mode of

conduct have this substantial and universally valid basis as their point of departure and result.[22]

Thus it appears that far from the state's being an entity that emerges from civil society, the reverse is closer to the case. Here Hegel makes it plain that his distinctive vision of the state is not an excuse to embrace authoritarianism; on the contrary, one can see a strong *communitarian* tendency in his thinking.

Civil society is the realm of need satisfaction, preference pursuit, and interpersonal interaction of the everyday sort, including commerce. Yet taken on its own, it is an arena in which particularity and discord threaten to overwhelm us and to eradicate civility. The endeavors of average citizens often come into conflict and differences between them sometimes fail to achieve arbitration and resolution. (Hegel would not, I think, be surprised at the competitiveness and litigiousness of today's society, especially in North America, but he would probably remind us forcefully that common purpose is more important than selfish gain and zero-sum games.[23]) Although antagonisms do not disappear within the state, there are mechanisms that help to ameliorate or eliminate these tensions. Voting, compensation for loss of one's property for the public good, and the administration of just punishment—deserved by someone whose will is invested in the laws—are three good examples of means by which animosities and differences are addressed. Beyond this, Hegel also calls attention to education (*Bildung*), which creates a culture of commonality, shared interests, and citizenship:

> It is part of education, of *thinking* as consciousness of the individual in the form of universality, that I am apprehended as a *universal* person, in which [respect] *all* are identical. A *human being counts as such because he is a human being*, not because he is a Jew, Catholic, Protestant, German, Italian, etc. This consciousness, which is the aim of *thought*, is of infinite importance, and it is inadequate only if it adopts a fixed position—for example, as *cosmopolitanism*—in opposition to the concrete life of the state.[24]

Hegel's central idea here, which strikes one as quite enlightened, is that the ability to identify with others gives each of us the universality we need to become who we want to be. As members of the state, we enjoy a maximum amount of freedom to construct ourselves in our own chosen manner and without interference, and we mutually endorse each other's projects of selfhood.

We can now understand why for Hegel, the state represents the presence of a rational principle in the world of interpersonal affairs and why we are therefore incomplete, as human individuals, apart from it. Attaining to a morally mature outlook, we open the way to being part of an egalitarian community with a history, common values, and shared purposes. And from the greatest degree of participation in the political process of the state flows not only the most significant individual and group benefits but also the most evolved form of personal freedom. The ideal human being, for Hegel, then, is one who engages fully with the ethical and political life of society, exercising the rights and responsibilities of citizenship. As well, he or she realizes personal aspirations in the daily commerce of civil society and is a loved and respected member of a family.

It remains only to note that Hegel found the most rational form of the state to be that of a constitutional monarchy (sections 275–86). This is because individuals participate in daily activities and in the political process as members of groups and as citizens of the realm; their particular selves have their desired universality within these collectives. The figure of the monarch, however, symbolizes that individuality is also paramount. When the state and the individual come into conflict, it is the state, as the concrete embodiment of everyone's will, that must prevail, yet it is still the individual will of the monarch that sanctions this result. In general, the monarch's final decisions serve to remind us and to reaffirm that the will of each discrete self is the foundation of the political entity that we call the state and that acts on our behalf.

Whether there ever was or ever will be a state that meets the criteria Hegel lays down is very uncertain. And there are, of course, defects in his own conception. But we have observed enough to discern that, contrary to what many have thought, Hegel was no mere idolater of the state in general, or of the repressive, militaristic Prussian state in particular. He makes this even more evident when he tells us, "The state is not a work of art; it exists in the world, and hence in the sphere of arbitrariness, contingency, and error, and bad behaviour may disfigure it in many respects. But the ugliest man, the criminal, the invalid, or the cripple is still a living human being; the affirmative aspect—life—survives in spite of such deficiencies, and it is with this affirmative aspect that we are here concerned."[25] And as we shall see in chapter 7, philosophy, for Hegel, of necessity understands only *what has been* and hence does not (or should not) preoccupy itself with either sanctifying the status quo or leading a charge into the future. Furthermore, he insists that the constitution is the outcome of a temporally lengthy process in which the spirit of a people is affirmed and expressed in a manner appropriate to it: "[A] constitution is not simply made: it is the work of centuries, the Idea and consciousness of the rational (in so far as that consciousness has developed in a nation)."[26] It is the universal will and the political culture of a nation that speaks through its constitution, expressing in it what individual selves together stand for. That being said, Hegel also cannot refrain from attributing some strange kind of divinity and ultrahuman origin to the constitution, notwithstanding its coming into being over a period of time.[27] The reason for this is that humans are always to be understood as the agents who bring the evolution of Absolute Spirit to its completion (see chapter 4).

HISTORY, FREEDOM, AND THE SELF AS AGENT

The remainder of this subdivision of the *Philosophy of Right* (sections 330–60) concerns itself with the interaction among states and outlines briefly the pattern of world history. The first of these themes is not germane to a consideration of the career of the self and so will not be pursued here; the second, however, we shall return to shortly in relation to the *Lectures on the Philosophy of World History*, where it is treated in much more detail by Hegel.

Recall that, like Aristotle, Hegel believed the universal is present in and inseparable from the particular, in humans as well as in everything else that exists. To manifest this universal, therefore—human excellence or humanity—is our unique gift and end as beings of the type we are. This is why Hegel says that "the destiny of individuals is to lead a universal life." It is this "universal life" that he identifies with the mature ethical order to which the state gives definition and with the most complete sort of freedom that emanates from a shared form of life. Hegel's pronouncements on the state's supreme position vis-à-vis human ethical and political life may nonetheless sound forbidding to some ears and even totalitarian in tone. Certainly, his writings did inspire theorists at both ends of the political spectrum and, truth be told, all points in between. But if we acquire some perspective, we will more readily understand why he assigns the functions that he does to the state. We need to place Hegel once again in the context of the social history of his time in order to grasp this matter properly.

According to historian J. Donald Hughes, "the vast majority of ancient people regarded themselves primarily as parts of their societies, and only secondarily, if at all, as individuals. Each person had a place in the social hierarchy which was rigidly defined and rarely changed."[28] Fortunately, this stultifying reality is no longer universal. Many human beings now experience their participation as members of society in a far different way. Philosopher Frederick A. Olafson observes, "As the objective possibilities of freely fashioning one's own life have increased, ideas of self-determination and of the necessity for a personal ratification by each individual of the mode of life proposed to him by his society have come to occupy a larger and larger place in the conception we form of ourselves."[29] Hegel was insecurely poised somewhere between these two worlds, in a period of accelerating change, and with tumultuous historical events occurring within his lifetime and looming on the not-too-distant horizon.

From the time of the Renaissance onward, the second picture had steadily taken over from the first. This process was enhanced by many factors that are familiar enough, but the one that weighed most heavily on his mind was the French Revolution. Hegel was a youthful enthusiast of this Revolution, but in later years, he began to worry about the anarchic energies released by it (as in the Reign of Terror) and feared the violent world events, modernizing tendencies, and social upheavals that he reasonably believed would be the price of any radically new political and social order. Consequently, he strived to work out a theory of the state that would allow for maximum personal liberty while at the same time guard against disunion, fragmentation, and harmful degrees of internal and external conflict. This helps to explain Hegel's position, even if it does not exonerate him from all charges of engaging in ways of thinking that could be construed as foreshadowing totalitarianism.

Such reflections as these naturally lead to a consideration of the individual's place in history, a topic of immense importance for Hegel. As I noted earlier (in chapter 1), Hegel was a historicist, that is, he believed all persons and their outlooks on the world are rooted in a unique place and time and are unintelligible in isolation from these. The self and all its projects of knowing and doing are social, hence defined by a particular era. But history possesses far greater significance than this, Hegel thought: It also has a *meaning*, we might even say a *plot*. This is because history is the concrete unfolding of Spirit's quest for self-expression and self-understanding. Humans participate in this process

—indeed, *they make it happen*. However, the larger context in which historical events occur is that of Absolute Spirit's self-realization. We can readily grasp, then, that for Hegel, it is in history that the mundane and cosmic concerns of his philosophy converge. The emergence of the self and its freedom, in social life and in the institutional and political life of the state, is also an episode of history in the broader sense.

Hegel's *Lectures on the Philosophy of World History* must be approached with some caution because (unlike the *Phenomenology of Spirit* and the *Philosophy of Right*) it is a posthumously published work composed of extracts from his own manuscripts and lecture notes but also of material taken from students' notes and editors' insertions. Thanks to meticulous scholarship, we can be fairly sure today that the work accurately represents Hegel's views, but in what follows, I rely as much as possible on those parts that are known to have been penned by the philosopher himself.

Without mincing words, Hegel informs his readers, "World history is the progress of the consciousness of freedom."[30] By this he means that history is where freedom emerges and becomes part of our common awareness. In a justly celebrated passage, he observes that in the ancient epoch of despots, pharaohs, god-kings, and autocrats, only *one* person is free in any meaningful sense, namely, the ruler. Even in the Greco-Roman world, only *some* individuals are free. (We like to recall ancient Greece as the birthplace of democracy, but only certain Athenian males—not women, slaves, or resident aliens—could claim full privileges of citizenship.[31]) He then asserts that "The *Germanic* [i.e., European] nations, with the rise of Christianity, were the first to realise that man is by nature free, and that freedom of the spirit is his very essence."[32] Hegel attributes to Jesus the (then) radical message that human beings are *each* of equal intrinsic value, *each* fully entitled to respect, love, and salvation. As I noted previously (in chapter 4), a major idea such as this, when unleashed, becomes the property of everyone and spreads like wildfire. It doesn't get universally accepted overnight but rather through a slow and circuitous process. This is the "progress of the consciousness of freedom" of which Hegel speaks, and which we still witness slowly and painfully unfolding.

Whether or not Hegel is correct about the origin of the concept that humans as such are free, there is no doubt that this idea *has* resulted from the moral and political evolution of our species and that it has ignited aspirations for liberty everywhere. What does it mean to say that "humans as such are free"? I think the answer is that self-determination (autonomy) is the implicit aim of human life, the route to self-actual-ization. We have to remember, however, that according to Hegel, freedom flowers fully only within the state. It can't be realized on one's own or on the level of private and limited interactions but solely within the context of citizenship and in a particular historical moment. Fur-thermore, freedom has to be worked for: Freedom "does not itself pos-sess an immediate and natural existence. It still has to be earned and won through the endless mediation of discipline acting upon the powers of cognition and will."[33] Quite simply, freedom does not just happen willy-nilly; it needs to be sought after, stimulated and nour-ished, through our active participation in the maturing experiences of life and in historical events.

The emergence of freedom in history furnishes many examples of dialectical change. We can take the civil rights movement in the United States during the 1950s and '60s as our focus. Much of this struggle was marred by violence and repression, directed at peaceful protesters, and by random, ugly acts of terrorism and intimidation perpetrated against average individuals going about their business, whose only "wrong-doing" was being African American. Demonstrations and acts of civil disobedience were met by police brutality and by threatening, con-frontational white mobs out of control. But in the long run, all of the attempts of the establishment to defend the status quo, to contain and eliminate the quest for full participation in society on the part of those who had been legally emancipated for a century, proved to be futile. And here is where we get to the Hegelian point: Violence, oppression, and ostracism, rather than accomplishing their objective (i.e., keeping African Americans in a quiescent, subordinate, disenfranchised posi-tion), *produced the opposite effect* to that which had been intended. Vio-lence defeated itself because of the backlash of public opinion and the power of the state to intervene.[34] As a result, an oppressed minority began to enjoy long-denied rights, such as freedom of movement, voting, and equal employment opportunities. The story is far from over, as we all know, but it does provide a good illustration of how collective behaviors that are designed to produce a certain outcome often subvert their own cause and yield—even accelerate into being—the reverse state of affairs. We can also say that this was an era in which the actions of average individuals made a difference to the course of events.

HISTORY'S TRAGIC SIDE

All of this sounds sensible, intriguing, uplifting, and perhaps even convincing. But there is a darker, more tragic vision embedded in Hegel's philosophy of history—one in which the career of the self seems to get lost or buried. He writes, for example, that "The dreams of the individual are often no more than exaggerated estimates of his own personal significance. Furthermore, the individual may well be treated unjustly; but this is a matter of indifference to world history, which uses individuals only as instruments to further its own progress."[35] He depicts history as an "altar on which the happiness of nations, the wisdom of states, and the virtue of individuals are slaughtered."[36] And, most gloomily of all, he avers that "history is not the soil in which happiness grows. The periods of happiness in it are the blank pages of history."[37]

What are we to make of all this? While it is true that ordinary people scarcely rate a mention in history texts, and bear all the sacrifices, don't they nonetheless play a significant role? Before we reach any conclusions, however, an additional element must be factored in. Lest we still suppose that average individuals really contribute to the direction of history, Hegel tells us that it is only "world-historical individuals" (like Alexander the Great, Caesar, and Napoléon) who make things happen. And even *they* are deluded about their own role, for it is "the cunning of reason" to use human agents' personal ambitions to carry out a larger purpose: "It sets the passions to work in its service, so that the agents by which it gives itself existence must pay the penalty and suffer the loss."[38] This notion of "the cunning of reason" (*List der Vernunft*) has been very controversial and its meaning is still highly problematic. Hegel could be saying one of several things: (a) that major historical figures just have the knack of seizing on what the times are ripe for and turning it into an opportunity, (b) that what these figures become obsessed with is the same as what the populace really wants but doesn't yet know it wants, (c) that what a world-historical individual unwittingly decides to do is identical to what he or she would have chosen if possessed of full consciousness of the decision factors that were pertinent at the time, or (d) that such a leader is merely a pawn of God, whose plan is the only game in town. We don't really know which of these doctrines Hegel intended, and there is textual support for each interpretation.

I think we must reluctantly conclude that there is a deep inconsistency here in Hegel's philosophy, in that it is individuals who are needed to make history move forward and not merely "world-histor-ical" individuals; the latter obviously can't do it alone. (This is the essential flaw in any "great man" account of history.) And as the example of the US civil rights movement showed, it is simply mistaken to believe that ordinary people don't count as historical agents. Yet it appears that for Hegel, in the end, *no one really matters*, only the result. It is as though the true subject of history is the Absolute or God. (Indeed, at one point Hegel remarks that "our investigation can be seen as a theodicy, a justification of the ways of God."[39]) We may attempt to lessen the impact of this depressing and odious conclusion by remem-bering that Hegel denies there is a gulf separating finite (human) Spirit from Absolute Spirit. We are all encompassed by the Absolute and have our being therein. This may provide some consolation. For many people *do* see their lives as contributing to, or being given meaning by, a higher purpose of some kind. Many others do *not* see things in this way, and for them what is important is that their lives should be signif-icant in *some* way, shape, or form. And those who hold the first view are obviously expressing the same desire. What disturbs us is the sense that Hegel may be knocking the props out from under our confidence that our personal selves *do* in fact matter. It seems that the cosmic perspec-tive has overshadowed the mundane one that he had so carefully built up. I don't believe there is any easy way to resolve this difficulty, and it helps account for why contemporary philosophers are much more interested in works like the *Phenomenology of Spirit* and the *Philosophy of Right* than in the *Lectures on the Philosophy of World History*.

HUMANS IN THE SOCIAL CONTEXT: HEGEL'S ACHIEVEMENT

Leaving aside the more obscure and perhaps outdated aspects of Hegel's philosophy of history, however, we can sum up his positive and lasting contribution. The self is a relational entity, constituted by its own efforts but also by its interaction with other selves, from which it acquires val-idation and gains in richness and depth. Complex forms of feedback exist in interpersonal relations, and these are formative influences on each of us. To say that the self is "socially constructed" does not mean that some reified entity, "society," shapes who and what we are; rather, it indicates that we achieve our identities in the presence of other persons with whom we are connected in one way or another from the start of life. As often as not, we must struggle for recognition and integrity, but this is part of the growth process. The joint activities of individuals give birth to society, which is an entity that emerges from many small- and large-scale interactions. Both individual selves and societies are located in historical settings, which also indelibly affect their identities. Participation in the family and civil society are vital to the career of the self. But full selfhood comes only with the rights, privileges, and obligations of state citizenship. As a member of the state, one acquires the political freedom that comes from the harmonious merging of wills in common goals that lie at the core of ethical life. The cohesiveness of the body politic is the source of true personhood.

We have here a sophisticated and in some ways quite appealing account of selfhood and good citizenship. Even if there are numerous points in his theory on which it would be more than reasonable to take issue with Hegel, there is arguably more in it that is of lasting value. A view of human life such as his, which stresses reciprocity at the personal level and a meaningful sense of community and collective purpose, is inspiring and will continue indefinitely to influence discussions in the field of social and political philosophy.

NOTES

1. G. W. F. Hegel, introduction to *Phenomenology of Spirit*, trans. A. V. Miller (Oxford: Clarendon Press, 1977), sec. 77, p. 49.

2. David Hume, "Of Personal Identity," in *A Treatise of Human Nature* (1739), ed. L. A. Selby-Bigge (Oxford: Clarendon Press, 1968), p. 252.

3. See Maurice Merleau-Ponty, "Hegel's Existentialism," in *Sense and Non-Sense*, by Maurice Merleau-Ponty, trans. Hubert L. Dreyfus and Patricia Allen Dreyfus (Evanston, IL: Northwestern University Press, 1964), pp. 63–70; and Robert C. Solomon, *From Hegel to Existentialism* (New York: Oxford University Press, 1987).

4. Hegel's claim that self-consciousness is contingent upon recognition is interestingly revisited by John Armstrong in *Conditions of Love: The Philosophy of Intimacy* (New York: Penguin Putnam, 2002), chap. 8.

5. See Michael Newton, *Savage Girls and Wild Boys* (London: Faber, 2002); Robert McGhee, "Co-evolution: New Evidence Suggests That to Be Truly Human Is to Be Partly Wolf," *Alternatives* 28, no. 1 (Winter 2002): 12–15; and Douglas Keith Candland, *Feral Children and Clever Animals: Reflections on*

Human Nature (Oxford: Oxford University Press, 1994). See also the following Web sites: www.feralchildren.com, http://en.wikipedia.org (search for "feral children"), and www.findarticles.com (online edition of *Gale Encyclopedia of Childhood and Adolescence*; search for "feral children"). Some famous feral children (real and fictional): Victor (the Wild Child of Aveyron), Kaspar Hauser, Romulus and Remus, Aegisthus, Mowgli, Tarzan, Pecos Bill, Davy Crockett.

6. Leo Buscaglia, *Love* (New York: Fawcett Crest, 1978), p. 81.

7. See Harry F. Harlow, *Learning to Love*, 2nd ed. (New York: Jason Aronson, 1974).

8. Hegel, *Phenomenology of Spirit*, trans. Miller, secs. 175, 177, p. 110.

9. Martin Heidegger, *Being and Time*, trans. John Macquarrie and Edward Robinson (London: SCM Press, 1962).

10. These ideas were especially stimulating to, and influential upon, the young Karl Marx. See, for example, his famous essay "Estranged Labor," in *Economic and Philosophic Manuscripts of 1844*, trans. Martin Milligan (Amherst, NY: Prometheus Books, 1988), pp. 69–84 (also readily available in many other translations and editions).

11. Many of these dynamics are analyzed and discussed in great detail by Jean-Paul Sartre in *Being and Nothingness: An Essay on Phenomenological Ontology*, trans. Hazel E. Barnes (New York: Philosophical Library, 1956), pt. 1, chap. 2, and pt. 3.

12. Jamie Crooks, "Understanding Desire," paper presented to a workshop on "Hegel on Desire and Recognition," Trent University, March 22–24, 2000.

13. G. W. F. Hegel, *Elements of the Philosophy of Right*, ed. Allen W. Wood, trans. H. B. Nisbet (Cambridge: Cambridge University Press, 1991), sec. 141, p. 185 (emphasis in original).

14. Ibid., sec. 21, p. 53 (emphasis in original).

15. Charles Taylor, *Hegel* (Cambridge: Cambridge University Press, 1975), p. 383. However, see pp. 160–61, and note 31 on p. 143 here.

16. Hegel, *Elements of the Philosophy of Right*, sec. 158, p. 199 (emphasis in original).

17. Ibid., sec. 256, p. 273 (emphasis in original).

18. Ibid., p. 274 (emphases in original).

19. Ibid., sec. 257, p. 275 (emphasis in original).

20. See T. M. Knox's translator's foreword to G. W. F. Hegel, *Philosophy of Right* (Oxford: Clarendon Press, 1958), p. x.

21. Hegel, *Elements of the Philosophy of Right*, sec. 183, p. 221 (emphasis in original).

22. Ibid., sec. 258, p. 276 (emphases in original).

23. See chapter 2, p. 43, for an explanation of zero-sum outcomes.

24. Hegel, *Elements of the Philosophy of Right*, sec. 209, p. 240 (emphases in original).

25. Ibid., sec. 258, p. 279.

26. Ibid., sec. 274, p. 313.

27. Ibid., sec. 273, p. 312.

28. J. Donald Hughes, *Ecology in Ancient Civilizations* (Albuquerque: University of New Mexico Press, 1975), p. 152.

29. Frederick A. Olafson, *Principles and Persons: An Ethical Interpretation of Existentialism* (Baltimore: Johns Hopkins Press, 1967), p. 238.

30. G. W. F. Hegel, *Reason in History*, trans. H. B. Hisbet (Cambridge: Cambridge University Press, 1975), p. 54. The word translated here as "Germanic" is *Germanisch*. Hegel does not use the word "German" (*Deutsch*) and thus avoids making a narrowly chauvinistic claim.

31. "Political rights were enjoyed only by men over eighteen years of age, born of Athenian parents enrolled in the citizen class," writes Walter R. Agard in *What Democracy Meant to the Greeks* (Chapel Hill: University of North Carolina Press, 1942), p. 69. Agard continues (p. 70), recording that "perhaps one-tenth of the total population had political rights."

32. Hegel, *Reason in History*, p. 54.

33. Ibid., pp. 98–99.

34. The following story is illuminating here. As a young man, Mohandas K. Gandhi campaigned against apartheid in South Africa. One day he had a meeting with the then very powerful Afrikaner General Jan Smuts. The very slight Gandhi said to him, "'I have come to tell you that I am going to fight against your government.' Smuts must have thought he was hearing things. 'You mean you have come here to tell me that?' he laughs. 'Is there anything more you want to say?' 'Yes,' says Gandhi. 'I am going to win.' Smuts is astonished. 'Well,' he says at last, 'and how are you going to do that?' Gandhi smiles. 'With your help.'" (Smuts acknowledged years later that Gandhi had spoken the truth.) The story is cited by E. Easwaran, *Gandhi the Man* (Petaluma, CA: Nilgiri Press, 1978).

35. Hegel, *Reason in History*, p. 65.

36. Ibid., p. 69.

37. Ibid., p. 79.

38. Ibid., p. 89.

39. Ibid., p. 42.

ISSUES AND OBSERVATIONS

HEGELIANISM

M y aim in this book has been to make Hegel's philosophy more accessible without oversimplifying it. I have tried to counteract the feeling of being at sea that one may get on first approaching Hegel so that the benefits of an acquaintance with his ideas can prevail instead. In this final chapter, I hope to show that it is possible to defend Hegel without being defensive and to be enriched by Hegelian thinking without having to be a Hegelian.

The synoptic sweep of Hegel's system, its majestic style of expression, and his dominant position in German philosophy exercised a powerful influence on nineteenth-century European intellectual life. For a brief period, his way of thinking completely dominated the agenda for debate among philosophers, social theorists, and religious thinkers, attracting some to his worldview and repelling others into reactive explorations of new theoretical territory. By general agreement among scholars of this period, there were three major strands of the early "Hegelianism" that flourished at this time. The principal contrast is between so-called Old and Young Hegelians. The orthodox Old Hegelians affirmed and embellished the master's synthesis of ideas, and several portrayed it as the most complete expression of Christianity. This group also refined and elaborated Hegel's position in the fields of ethics, legal studies, aesthetics, and the history of philosophy. Its members are largely forgotten today, but their most significant contribution was undoubtedly the editing of the first comprehensive collection of Hegel's works. Of greater interest, importance, and influence were the Young Hegelians.

The Young Hegelians (sometimes called "Neo-Hegelians") are classified into "left-wing" and "right-wing" movements, both of which lasted from approximately 1830 to 1848. As might be inferred from the label, left-wing Hegelians seized upon the radical or revolutionary impulse in Hegel's thought, while right-wing Hegelians opted for the defense of constitutional monarchy and the compatibility of Hegel's philosophy with their own novel interpretations of Christianity. (A Hegelian "center," comprising philosophers who attempted to reconcile these opposing camps, also can be discerned.) On the left were situated several well-known figures, such as Ludwig Feuerbach, Karl Marx, and Friedrich Engels, and their less renowned associates Arnold Ruge, Max Stirner, David Strauss, and others. Their work consisted mainly of deconstructing and demythologizing religion, which they believed to be a human response to deep psychological needs that are not met adequately within the social sphere, and of envisioning a new, egalitarian political order. Because Hegel had emphasized the restless and fluid aspects of thought and reality, they assumed that any barrier to change could be overcome and that the tide of progress could be turned in a chosen direction by those who properly understood the dynamics of history. On the right have been placed Bruno Bauer and (sometimes) Søren Kierkegaard. Thinkers of this stripe tended to be politically and theologically conservative, though in many ways quite radical in their critiques, not only of Hegel, but also of contemporary institutions. However, the left/right division, while suggestive and perhaps of some value, is not particularly reliable, as several authors have pointed out,[1] owing to the varying allegiances of the Young Hegelians on different issues, and to the development of each as an independent thinker.

PHILOSOPHY IN THE REARVIEW MIRROR

This polarized perspective on the aftermath of Hegel's career nevertheless helps us appreciate the controversial nature of his legacy and provides a framework for reflecting on his philosophical achievement. One of Hegel's most memorable and enigmatic pieces of prose, which many readers may recognize, is the following:

> A further word on the subject of *issuing instructions* on how the world ought to be: philosophy, at any rate, always comes too late to perform this function. As the *thought* of the world, it appears only at a time when actuality has gone through its formative process and attained its complete state. This lesson of the concept is necessarily also apparent from history, namely that it is only when actuality has reached maturity that the ideal appears opposite the real and reconstructs this real world, which it has grasped in its substance, in the shape of an intellectual realm. When philosophy paints its grey in grey, a shape of life has grown old, and it cannot be rejuvenated, but only recognized, by the grey in grey of philosophy; the owl of Minerva begins its flight only with the onset of dusk.[2]

We learn from both philosophy and history, in other words, that the world can be understood only retrospectively, that is, looking backward from the present. Events that are still unfolding have not yet exhausted their energies and fully expressed their potential for bringing about change. Interpretation and explanation always lie in the future, with respect to the present, and in the present, with respect to the past. Hence systematic philosophy is limited in its horizon, and mature wisdom, figuratively speaking, comes to us, if at all, only at the end of the day. Furthermore, we cannot look to philosophy for practical guidance as to conduct in the social and political realms.

Hegel's oracular pronouncement seems to imply that all we can hope for in philosophy is the classification and organization in thought of a world that is dead and gone. (Philosophers, in short, like armchair generals and quarterbacks, always speak with the benefit of hindsight.) If he is right, not only can no one succeed in comprehending the present; it is just as futile to project into the future any intelligible trends that can direct our behavior and hopeless for us to try controlling what will go on there. Yet even if one sometimes feels today that things really *are* this way, I would argue that most of us don't in fact believe that our view of the future is so limited, and furthermore, we can scarcely lead our lives in accordance with such a notion. It is hard to imagine that Hegel sincerely endorsed his own thesis, in his heart of hearts. But at the very least it seems inescapable that he is cautioning us against expecting philosophy to explain current trends in detail or to help us actively change the future. If so, utopian visions are for naught and we might as well turn our attentions elsewhere.

In a related text, Hegel compounds our puzzlement when he states:

> Philosophy begins with the decline of a real world. . . . What it produces, then, is a remedy, but only in the world of thought, not in the earthly world. . . . Thus, the Greeks, when they began to think, withdrew from the state; and they began to think at a time when in the world around them there was nothing but turbulence and wretchedness, e.g., during the time of the Peloponnesian War. . . . So it has been with almost all peoples: philosophy makes its first appearance when public life is no longer satisfying.[3]

This position strikes one as remarkably similar to Marx's indictment of philosophy for its failure to do any real work in our lives.[4] It also seems at odds with the exalted place Hegel assigns to philosophy in his hierarchy of human cultural achievements. How are these discrepancies to be accounted for? The answer, I believe, is fairly complex and also ultimately unsatisfying. Each culture has its era of vitality, during which it expresses its creative impulse with spontaneous vigor. But it has its phase of disintegration as well. That is when philosophy flourishes because it is in the realm of thought that the human spirit regroups and gains strength for a new leap forward. But it is not that philosophy *leads* the advance; rather, philosophy *sums up and analyzes what has been* so that the "truth" of what has been can be extracted. The past can then contribute to the present's way of confronting the future.

Viewed from this angle, we see that Hegel's claim is very different from Marx's pragmatist argument concerning the impotence of philosophy. Moreover, it looks as if we must interpret Hegel as making an exception to the rule for his own philosophical system. The reason is that he holds it to be not the expression of decadence but rather, as we have seen, the apex of human cultural evolution, the highest development of Spirit. Now if his system *is* to be judged differently, then he can argue that Absolute Idealism is *both* the owl of Minerva taking off into the dusk *and* a dynamic achievement that resonates with special significance for humankind as a whole. Whether this self-assessment should go unchallenged is an open question. *If* we accept Hegel's theory that his system is the capstone of the history of philosophy, this would seem to place his contribution in a class by itself, as an anomalous and triumphant form of philosophizing. But few have been willing to grant him this much, and without such a concession, Hegel's philosophical enterprise appears to be in mortal danger from its own unresolved internal tensions.

THE RATIONAL AND THE ACTUAL: HEGEL'S PROGRESSIVISM

We have just been witnessing the conservative side of Hegel, where it seems that attempts to bring about historical and political changes, such as improving the lot of disadvantaged people, are pointless. If that is the case, then ought we to adapt to the status quo, perhaps seeing in it the best that our society or humanity at large can do? Such an interpretation may be supposed to draw strength from another well-known Hegelian phrase, "What is rational is actual; and what is actual is rational."[5] On the surface, it appears that Hegel here glorifies or at least condones whatever state of affairs currently exists. If what is rational is actual and vice versa, then there is no criticizing the way things are; we might just as well accept them and get on with our lives. This could even extend to not questioning authority, not trying to bring about social reforms, and so on. Did Hegel really mean this? The phrase I have quoted comes from the *Philosophy of Right*. It appears again in an edition of the *Encyclopedia of the Philosophical Sciences* (part 1) that was published later, and we see that he is already reacting to criticisms of his doctrine that are based on misunderstandings. In the *Encyclopedia*, Hegel retorts: "These simple statements have given rise to expressions of surprise and hostility, even in quarters where it would be reckoned an insult to presume absence of philosophy, and still more of religion."[6] He goes on to explain his meaning in this way: No thing and no state of affairs is fully intelligible and realized unless and until its essence coincides with its existence, that is, only if and when it adequately expresses the universal of which it is the instantiation. Elsewhere, he gives some examples to illustrate the point:

> The state is actual, and its actuality consists in the fact that the interest of the whole realizes itself through the particular ends. Actuality is always the unity of universality and particularity, the resolution of universality into particularity; the latter then appears to be self-sufficient, although it is sustained and supported only by the whole. If this unity

is not present, nothing can be *actual*, even if it may be assumed to have *existence*. A bad state is one which merely exists; a sick body also exists, but it has no true reality. A hand which has been cut off still looks like a hand and exists, but it has no actuality.[7]

Thus, something is actual ("true" or genuine) when it coincides with, functions in accordance with, or fully expresses its concept or manifests its essence. Prior to that time, or apart from that condition, therefore, it is not "rational," according to Hegel. So what is truly intelligible (rational) in the world is that which completely displays its potential (has become actual). And what instantiates the universal adequately (i.e., is actual) is something thought can grasp and assimilate without contradiction (i.e., is rational).

As I have had occasion to remark previously, a concept, in Hegel's sense, is an active essence that is embedded in individual things (the "concrete universal" we have previously met with), making them become what they are meant to be. This idea is markedly different from that which is fairly standard in both ordinary thinking and philosophy, namely, that a concept is merely a general notion abstracted from experience of, or thinking about, particulars. For this reason, translators often capitalize Hegel's special usage of "Concept" (*Begriff*) in order to flag its extra meaning.

If we are on the right track, then it appears much less clear that Hegel *is* justifying the status quo in the world. For it is open to him to say (as indeed he does say) that we still have a long way to go before what is and what ought to be coincide. Freedom, for instance, is not actual until it is fully realized in the world, in the institutions and ways of life of a culture—and eventually worldwide. The idea is out and about that everyone is free and equal, but no society on earth gives universal expression to this concept. Thus, they all still fall short of being rational and actual in Hegel's terms. The important next step is that we are invited by the logic of his theory to suppose future developments might bring us to the point where rationality and actuality will prevail and indeed become equivalent, where the established order will have given way to a dramatically different state of affairs. And this certainly seems anything but a conservative or quietist position.

Add to this Hegel's characterization of the dialectic as "the genuine nature that properly belongs to the determinations of the understanding, to things, and to the finite in general," and it is easy to cast him as a subversive, even revolutionary thinker.[8] For if dialectical reasoning, and even more so, the force of dialectic in the fabric of the world, have this kind of power, then anything can happen or perhaps be made to happen. This kind of approach gave a big boost to those who would interrogate present values and realities, convinced as they were that Hegel could be coopted in support of developing strategies for social, political, and religious transformation.

And finally, recent Hegelian scholarship has disclosed that our philosopher sought to avoid censorship of his *Philosophy of Right* by assuring any officials who might be reading it "that his philosophy of the state contains nothing dangerous or subversive"—which undoubtedly means he realized that it does. Furthermore, Hegel intervened on behalf of several students and academic colleagues at the University of Jena who were being persecuted for their political activities. As well, a prominent French liberal who knew him personally remarks that Hegel "considered the French Revolution to be the greatest step forward taken by humanity since Christianity" and was himself "profoundly liberal."[9]

Viewing this other, impatiently reformist side of Hegel makes us understand better how he could have inspired radical thinkers of his own time and later. It also stimulates us to ponder another issue: What was the likely future that Hegel envisioned for his *own* philosophy? But beyond this, whatever Hegel may have thought, what account of the matter may plausibly be drawn from his writings? The reason these questions arise is that if we can identify a strong impulse toward transformation in Hegel's philosophy, we want to know whether this may have a fateful impact not only upon the world around us but upon his own thought product as well. Lawrence Stepelevich claims that Hegel believed his own philosophical system could *not* be superseded, and if correct, this interpretation would be consistent with Stepelevich's assignment of Hegel himself to the Old Hegelians.[10] However, I would argue that it is equally compelling to conclude that Hegel's philosohy *encourages its own demise*, or rather, its own dialectical absorption by a more advanced system. Certainly the Young Hegelians saw things that way. They might not have been so concerned with finding textual support for their stance (though as we have seen there is some), but we can hardly fault them for discovering the radical core of Hegel's thought—which quite probably even Hegel himself did not see very clearly.

PARADOXES OF THE ABSOLUTE

Other intriguing questions remain about Hegel's philosophy and his achievement. One concerns his peculiar metanarrative of Absolute Spirit's self-realization. As we have seen, Hegel portrays the Absolute as needing to go through stages of self-estrangement or self-alienation and to overcome these in order to attain to full expression and completeness. This is, in some sense, the plan of the world. Humans participate in this plan in finite ways and within their own limited context also pass through stages of self-alienation and de-alienation. At both levels, a dialectical progression is operative; opposed aspects of the self, self and world, or self and other become subsumed in a more encompassing and richer result, as when individual wills merge in society or when the allegedly independent subject and object of knowledge come to be viewed, not as separate, but as mutually determining and relational. However, the following question might be raised: Why does the Absolute (or God) have to go through these stages in order to become Absolute? Surely the creative force in the cosmos either is or is not Absolute, or complete and self-sufficient, the total fulfilment of everything it can be.

The same question, or type of question, naturally arises in connection with forms of theism that are more standard and traditional than Hegel's quite unusual brand. For example, most theists at some point confront questions like these: Who made God? What was there before God? Why did God need to create anything if he is complete and perfect? Where does evil come from if God is all-good? Where does Satan get his power from if God is omnipotent? Of these, the third is most similar to the question we are now confronting. There are many possible answers that could be offered in order to preserve the intelligibility and rational consistency of a theistic belief system. I am interested at the moment only in Hegel's response, and I suggest that it goes something like this: The best way to understand the universe overall, and our world in particular, is to conceptualize them as purposefully evolving, that is, as comprising a continuous development, made up of gradual changes but also moving toward an end-state of some kind. God is the energizing force in all this (the "subject" behind it, as it were) and also its manifestations (the collectivity of created entities, or "substance") that we encounter and indeed are part of. This outlook is what identifies Hegel as a process philosopher, one who sees the universe in terms of happenings rather than things and properties, discrete events, and so on. Saying so does not entail that things and such are illusory, for Hegel never makes this sort of claim. His alternative is to offer a more fluid method of understanding reality, which we have explored in some detail in earlier chapters.

So, then, let's return to The Big Question: Why *does* the Absolute need to externalize and then recover itself in order to become fully actual (and hence, fully rational)? Why does it need to pass through the phases of self-alienation, finding itself dismembered in the other, then reuniting with itself? Simply because this is the general pattern according to which all movement, change, and development occur. First, there is a configuration of such and such an identifiable sort. Then, there is a movement away from this configuration (negation). Finally, a new identity establishes itself that incorporates elements of the preceding stages (negation of negation plus advance). A new cycle follows, and the entire process continues until all of its inner contradictions have been overcome. Explaining God or the Absolute, therefore, amounts to explaining reality on the most general level at which we can attempt an account of anything. If it is a fundamental fact of experience that nature (in the most universal sense) is dynamic and temporal rather than static, any explanation we give must start from there and be adequate to these data. And if we inhabit a cosmos rather than a chaos, it makes sense to attempt a systematic explanation of reality that is faithful to the flow of becoming but yet finds unity and wholeness in this flow.

HEGEL AND HIS CRITICS: A DEFENSE

We now come face-to-face with another difficult problem, which is whether a philosophical system such as Hegel's is possible at all. This question may be interpreted in a number of ways, so it would be best to settle at the outset what it is we are up against here. It might be thought that the question is whether anyone can master all of knowledge today, as allegedly could be done in the Renaissance period. Was Hegel, perhaps, a "Renaissance Man" of his era? This is *not* the question that is before us. Hegel was very learned and his works spanned an incredible spectrum of concerns. Much of his information, however, was incomplete, inadequate, or flawed, even if it was the best available to him, and his opinions betrayed the biases of his time (e.g., his views that Asia, Africa, and Latin America are doomed to play no further part in history and that all other religions are inferior to Christianity). We no longer believe anyone can aspire to be a Renaissance Man (or Woman), with knowledge having grown exponentially in the past century. And even if Hegel had been a Renaissance Man of his time, he would not and could not be of ours.

Nor is the question just one concerning whether Hegel's synthesis of ideas remains credible today. There can be, and there are, Hegelians, but vanishingly few, I should think, that truly believe Hegel said it all. Even his most loyal followers in the nineteenth century still wrote their own books and developed their own positions. And we have seen that one can find much that is of value in Hegel without having to buy it all.[11]

While this second approach to the question does get us a bit closer to the heart of the matter, we still need to take a different tack. The central issue, I believe, is whether philosophy, and any practitioner of it, can credibly paint the universe with the broad brush and selective palette that Hegel does. This problem has been spotlighted in different ways, of which a sample follows. Kierkegaard, one of Hegel's most vociferous and dogged critics, argues at great length that the experience of existence (the true subject matter of philosophy, he contends) cannot be subsumed or explained by philosophy; therefore, *any* philosophical system is doomed to incompleteness and absurdity insofar as it violates this premise. Here is a taste of his prose and dry satirical criticism:

> I am as willing as anyone to fall down in worship before the system if I could only catch a glimpse of it. . . . A few times I have been very close to worshiping, but behold, at the very moment I had already spread my handkerchief on the ground, so as to avoid dirtying my trousers by kneeling, when I for the last time very innocently said to one of the initiates, "Now, tell me honestly, is it indeed completely finished, because if that is the case, I will prostrate myself, even if I should ruin a pair of trousers" (on account of the heavy traffic to and from the system, the road was rather muddy)—I would invariably receive the answer, "No, it is not entirely finished yet." And so the system and the kneeling were postponed once again. . . . Existence itself is a system—for God, but it cannot be a system for any existing spirit. . . . Existence is the spacing that holds apart; the systematic is the conclusiveness that combines. . . . Existence must be annulled in the eternal before the system concludes itself.[12]

A century later, Karl Jaspers (1883–1969) characterized the generation of philosophers after Kant (including Hegel) as spinning out "speculative constructions, intellectual visions in which they tell us what God was thinking before and during the Creation. . . . Casting off Kant's humility, these philosophers thought the thoughts of God."[13] And contemporary historian of philosophy D. W. Hamlyn complains:

> There is an overweening arrogance in Hegel's claim to have produced a complete map of all possible knowledge and of reality. The same applies to Hegel's view that reality is revealed to, and indeed constituted by, a self or spirit which is universal and such that individual selves and their thoughts are just individual aspects or "moments" of it. . . . Many have seen in the attempts at system and comprehensiveness a form of paranoia.[14]

In various ways and styles, these authors are united in objecting to Hegel's claims of comprehensiveness and finality for his philosophy. They also accuse him of inexcusable hubris for supposing he can discern the overall shape of reality from a superior standpoint. Let us try to get a grip on what these charges amount to.

First of all, Kierkegaard did not reject Hegel's dialectical view of existence; he in fact assumed it in his own original theory (Existentialism). But where he adamantly parts company with Hegel is over the ability of rational thought to embrace existence and order it logically. He thinks that Hegel begins and ends arbitrarily and that any pretense at completeness on the part of Absolute Idealism is simply a farce. We may agree that Kierkegaard has a point: There is much about life that is mysterious and eludes our attempts to understand, let alone systematize. A healthy approach to the art of living will therefore have to center on choice and decisiveness in the face of uncertainty. But in a way, because Kierkegaard has such a different agenda from Hegel, and such an utterly opposing conception of what philosophy is (or should be) all about, there is little gain in trying to rescue Hegel from this attack. Anyone can say of Kierkegaard, "He's right, Hegel's wrong." (Or, for that matter, "Hegel's on the money, Kierkegaard's out to lunch.") But aside from the fact that this kind of declaration does not amount to an argument, there are indefinitely many philosophers among whom people may choose in a similar spirit. Yet we all have reasons for preferring the philosophy that we do, even if we haven't articulated them consciously. Be that as it may, it also needs to be recognized that while Hegel did believe in the possibility of a reasoned interpretation of all reality, he was not blind or insensitive to the ambiguities and ordeals of everyday life. He would be the first to impress upon us the notion that we are all in the position of having to overcome our dogmatic assumptions and limited outlooks in order to gain a vision of wholeness. And this is both painful and takes time—lots of time.

Jaspers's comment on Hegel (and others) is something of a caricature. We might superficially fault Hegel for assuming a "God's-eye view" of the universe, like the numerous past systematic philosophers and Romantic contemporaries he criticizes for their hasty intuitions of the whole. But it would behoove us to pause and ask ourselves whether this is indeed what he is doing. I would respond that he does *not* take such a stance. While he has a vision of his own, he painstakingly creates a rational reconstruction of it. In so doing, he builds up, incrementally, a picture that purports to make better sense of the world we experience, and of the relation between God and world, than any rival hypothesis.[15] He may wrongly judge his achievement a success according to this criterion, but if so, it would remain to demonstrate either that the criterion itself is faulty (Kierkegaard) or that his system has not fully or adequately accomplished the task (later Idealist philosophers, such as F. H. Bradley and J. M. E. McTaggart). And neither is an easy assignment.

As far as Hamlyn is concerned, the remarks I have cited seem to be in part based on a misapprehension of what Hegel was up to and in part nothing more than crude character assassination. Hegel did not contend that he had "produced a complete map of all possible knowledge and of reality." To begin with, he never said this. And the fact that he praised and encouraged his first generation of followers (the Old Hegelians) in their efforts to develop Absolute Idealist philosophy proves the point.[16] Hegel reiterates many times that no one can know everything, especially how the future will unfold. There are always unpredictable dialectical backwaters on the way to higher insight, and the social and political world we inhabit is still very far from being hospitable to the satisfaction of humans' potential. Beyond this, we may agree that there is a problem about the subsumption of individuals into the universal self or Spirit (the Absolute or God), but this is not unique to Hegel; it is an aspect of every mystical consciousness or variant of panentheism that has yet been espoused. Hegel's relegation of humans to the position of being the cannon fodder of history strikes us as especially reprehensible. But the idea that we are all part of God, that God infuses each person with spirit, surely deserves something more than mere dismissal. Finally, to attribute "overweening arrogance" and "paranoia" to Hegel is little more than a retreat into an ad hominem (an attack on the person rather than the message). I believe I have offered a more plausible suggestion concerning the possible origin of Hegel's metaphysics in chapter 3, tracing it to a fundamental awareness of some kind. If I am correct, we may still consider his outlook too grandiose and his expression of it too pompous, but we would be approaching it quite differently (and more constructively) in formulating these conclusions. On one point, however, we certainly must agree with Hamlyn: "It is not surprising that it [Hegel's philosophy] produced heated reactions."

On another theme—Hegel's legendary difficulty and obscurity— there are many whom we might cite. Most amusing and acerbic, however, is Arthur Schopenhauer (1788-1860):

> But the greatest effrontery in serving up sheer nonsense, in scrabbling together senseless and maddening webs of words, such as had previously been heard only in madhouses, finally appeared in Hegel. It became the instrument of the most ponderous and general mystification that has ever existed, with a result that will seem incredible to posterity, and be a lasting monument of German stupidity.[17]

Elsewhere, Schopenhauer adds further insult to injury, calling Hegel "a commonplace, inane, loathsome, repulsive, and ignorant charlatan," and charging, "The extensive intellectual activity that was forcibly usurped by such a man resulted in the mental ruin of a whole generation of scholars. The admirer of this pseudophilosophy has in store for him the ridicule of posterity."[18] All of this remarkably persistent slander has prompted one scholar to observe shrewdly that "Hegel is merely Schopenhauer's antagonistic brother, closely bound to him in negation."[19]

Schopenhauer was an outstanding philosopher but also a malicious and embittered individual who failed as an academic and also fell short of the fame he thought he deserved until late in life. It didn't help for him to stubbornly schedule his own lectures at the University of Berlin, purely out of spite, so that they coincided with those being delivered by the already renowned and charismatic Hegel. Hegel, who actually helped his miserable and ungrateful compatriot obtain a lectureship, rode out the storm of invective, as might be expected.

It must once again be acknowledged that there is a point behind the torrent of verbal abuse and the unworthy posturing. There is no disputing that a large amount of Hegel's writing *is* impenetrable and unintelligible to many people, native German speakers included. Why is this, and couldn't he have done better to reach out to his audience? Of course, part of the answer hinges on who his audience was meant to be. This is debatable, but Hegel did, for example, write his *Encyclopedia of the Philosophical Sciences* for undergraduate university students as a kind of "compendium" of his system.[20] This purpose notwithstanding, as the most recent translators of this work lament, "Many a sentence, 'like a wounded snake, drags its slow length along'. Then there is Hegel's unique vocabulary, which involved giving ordinary German words new or at least specialised meanings, inventing new expressions, and deliberately exploiting the special capacity of the German language for neologisms."[21] Perhaps more felicitous are Hegel's celebrated series of lectures on diverse subjects, to which I have referred numerous times.

What can be said here on behalf of our philosopher? Why didn't he just say what he meant? To be sure, Hegel *did* say what he meant, the question being whether he said it clearly enough. And I would be the first to concede that he did not, otherwise the need for the book you are reading would not be so urgent. I would also add that we cannot fully exonerate him on this particular score. There is no doubt that philosophy is a difficult subject, and everyone who has ever taken it up seriously will agree that it is really hard to say things with precision; the biggest task, in fact, may just be that of "getting it right." What one means is always hanging in the balance, awaiting the verdict of others as to whether it has been communicated successfully. But to be generous to Hegel, it must be observed that he was attempting to do something unprecedented, bringing to light things that are extraordinarily subtle and elusive. He was attempting to create a way of talking about the inner rhythm of a constantly changing world, and his overall endeavor was to demonstrate the organic, integrated, seamless, evolving nature of reality. It is one thing to characterize these aims in very general terms, as I have just done, but it is quite another to work them out in the excruciating detail that is required in order to illustrate the point, be persuasive, and attain completeness. And as poets, artists, and original thinkers other than Hegel would hasten to amplify, when trying to say something that is really fresh and groundbreaking, it is often necessary to invent a new "language" for the purpose. The onus is then on the audience to interpret what it encounters, feeling its way gingerly into the work. For Hegel, the invention of a new language is both metaphorically and literally operative, and coming to terms with it is a challenge-cum-obstacle that we can only do our best to surmount. A frequently cumbersome style presents additional perils. This is the negative side of the matter; the positive side is that we learn and become more sophisticated as we progress, and this achievement rewards our understanding in proportion to the time devoted to the task. The same is true of the study of any subject. We have to master the vocabulary, the concepts, the explanatory framework, the method. Schopenhauer didn't think there was anything in Hegel that merited this amount of devotion and expenditure of energy. But, leaving aside his mean-spirited personal vendetta, the most plausible explanation of this attitude is that he had his own, very different and in some ways antithetical, philosophical approach to try to market against heavy odds. *We* need not choose between Hegel and Schopenhauer, however; to the degree we see fit, we can take the time to enjoy both thinkers, and others besides.

HEGEL'S STORY OF HUMAN DESTINY

I will close this set of reflections on Hegel's philosophy with a look at one final issue: whether there is any justification for his belief that social and historical developments are progressive, that there is a goal toward which our species' life is heading. This is another way of questioning whether his metanarrative is, in the end, convincing.

The belief in human progress as a kind of destiny is out of fashion, but it was very much in vogue in Hegel's day.[22] Even Marx, who resembled Schopenhauer in respect to the contempt for Hegel he vented through his writings, nonetheless shared the belief that progress is, or at least could be, the lot of human beings. It is difficult to pin Marx down on this point, which is why I've said "is, or at least could be." His account of past history is certainly progressive. But with respect to the future, he is more ambivalent. On the one hand, Marx asserts that capitalism will develop to its limit, then succumb to its own inner "contradictions," thereby opening a vista toward the utopian communist world to come. This chain of events appears almost inevitable. On the other hand, it seems the workers of the world (proletarians) must seize the reins of history in order to make this kind of future possible, in which case utopia is not inevitable, though it can be won through struggle. Of one thing Marx *was* sure, and that is that Hegel's dialectic must be inverted to get at the truth:

> My dialectic method is not only different from the Hegelian, but its direct opposite. To Hegel, the life-process of the human brain, i.e., the process of thinking, which, under the name of "the Idea," he even transforms into an independent subject, is the demiurgos [prime mover] of the real world, and the real world is only the external, phenomenal form of "the Idea." With me, on the contrary, the ideal is nothing else than the material world reflected by the human mind, and translated into forms of thought. . . . The mystification which dialectic suffers in Hegel's hands, by no means prevents him from being the first to present its general form of working in a comprehensive and conscious manner. With him it is standing on its head. It must be turned right side up again, if you would discover the rational kernel within the mystical shell.[23]

For Marx, the material conditions of existence (natural resources, basic need satisfaction, technology, the relations of production, etc.) come first, and all else flows from them. Ideas are not primary formative factors in history, being part of the derivative "superstructures" of society; that is, they are effects more than causes of anything. (This is a paradoxical claim, given the huge contribution Marx's own ideas have made to bringing about historical change.) Hegel had discovered a certain truth (the dialectical nature of things), says Marx, but communicated it in a garbled fashion. His message therefore had to be decoded before it could become useful. To engineer a revolution, then, requires transformation of the material basis of human life, not tinkering with ideas.

But Hegel, as we have found throughout, held otherwise. Ideas unleashed on humankind make all the difference to what happens, even if the path to our collective goal—the convergence of the rational and the actual—is a tortuous and torturous one. Progress is discernible by those who know what to seek, as Hegel remarks: "Whoever looks at the world rationally will find that it in turn assumes a rational aspect."[24] The pattern is there even if the details are lacking.

Whether the history of our species is marked by progress is an enormous question that cannot be pursued in depth here. Furthermore, it all depends, as philosophers like to say, on what you mean by "progress." Clearly knowledge (and even more so, information) is pro-

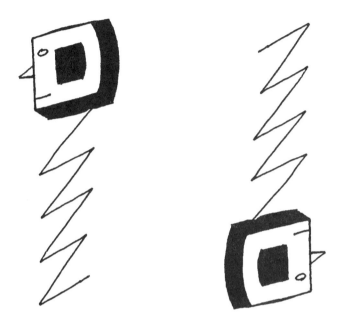

Hegel's dialectic: rightside up or upside down?

gressive, that is, cumulative, and expanding all the time. What is much more troubling to contemplate is whether there is any reason to believe in such a thing as moral progress. Looking out on the world as I write (during the US-led invasion and occupation of Iraq) does not invite immediate encouragement on this score. Yet Hegel had great faith in the human spirit and a long-range optimism without which we today can hardly dispense with, if we want to have a decent psychological survival kit. And who is to say he was wrong to affirm that one day rationality will triumph over irrationality, that we will have met the enemy—which is us—and conquered it, once and for all? Either way, in the end, as Hegel would say, "World history is the world's court of judgment."[25]

What we learn from these reflections is that Hegel was a pivotal figure in the transition from modernism to postmodernism. If modernism can be characterized by, among other things, belief in the inevitability of progress in human affairs, the viability of grand narratives about reality, and the legitimacy of authoritative pronouncements on matters of universal significance to humanity, then Hegel can be seen as one of its last great representatives. But inasmuch as he questions foundationalism in epistemology, the prevalence of rationality in human practices, any basis for planning the future, and strongly advocates historicism, he wears the mantle of postmodernism. Thus Hegel remains a contradiction in his own right—an endless source of inspiration and controversy, a thinker ever inviting appropriation and reinterpretation.

NOTES

1. See, for example, Lawrence S. Stepelevich, ed., *The Young Hegelians: An Anthology* (London: Cambridge University Press, 1983), pp. 9 ff.; John Edward Toews, *Hegelianism: The Path Toward Dialectical Humanism, 1805–1841* (Cambridge: Cambridge University Press, 1980), pp. 203–207. The whole structure of Karl Loewith's *From Hegel to Nietzsche: The Revolution in Nineteenth-Century Thought*, trans. David E. Green (New York: Holt, Rinehart and Winston, 1964), illustrates the point as well.

2. G. W. F. Hegel, preface to *Elements of the Philosophy of Right*, ed. Allen W. Wood, trans. H. B. Nisbet (Cambridge: Cambridge University Press, 1991), p. 23 (emphases in original).

3. G. W. F. Hegel, introduction to *Lectures on the History of Philosophy*, in Quentin Lauer, *Hegel's Idea of Philosophy* (New York: Fordham University Press, 1971), p. 98.

4. Marx reacted to this by saying, in effect, "If philosophy can't change the world, then let's find something else that can, perhaps economics and polemics." As he famously asserted, "The philosophers have only *interpreted* the world, in various ways; the point is to *change* it." Marx seldom allowed that philosophy has a role *of any kind* in changing the world, or that interpretation comes prior to action (as it must be), preferring instead to trash philosophy, as in the following priceless remark: "Philosophy and the study of the actual world have the same relation to one another as masturbation and sexual love." The quotations are from "Theses on Feuerbach," XI (emphasis in original), p. 123, and *The German Ideology*, p. 103, respectively, both to be found in C. J. Arthur, ed., *The German Ideology and Supplementary Texts*, 2nd ed. (London: Lawrence and Wishart, 1977).

5. Hegel, preface to *Elements of the Philosophy of Right*, p. 20.

6. G. W. F. Hegel, *Hegel's Logic*, trans. William Wallace, 3rd ed. (Oxford: Clarendon Press, 1975), sec. 6, p. 9.

7. Hegel, *Elements of the Philosophy of Right*, sec. 270, addition, p. 302 (emphases in original). Hegel's last example is taken from Aristotle.

8. G. W. F. Hegel, *Encyclopaedia Logic*, trans. T. F. Geraets, W. A. Suchting, and H. S. Harris (Indianapolis: Hackett, 1991), sec. 81, p. 128.

9. Allen W. Wood, editorial notes in Hegel, *Elements of the Philosophy of Right*, no. 6, p. 383, and no. 12, p. 386. Victor Cousin (1792–1867) makes his remarks in "Souvenirs d'Allemagne," *Revue de deux mondes* (August 1866): 616–17.

10. Stepelevich, ed., *Young Hegelians*, p. 4.

11. The view that Hegel himself would not be a Hegelian today is explored in some respects in Emil L. Fackenheim and James A. Doull, "Would Hegel Today Be a Hegelian?" *Dialogue* 9 (1970): 222–35.

12. Søren Kierkegaard, *Concluding Unscientific Postscript to Philosophical Fragments*, trans. Howard V. Hong and Edna H. Hong, vol. 1 (Princeton, NJ: Princeton University Press, 1992), pp. 107, 118, 122.

13. Karl Jaspers, *Kant* (*The Great Philosophers*, vol. 1), trans. Ralph Manheim (New York: Harcourt, Brace and World, 1962), pp. 151, 152.

14. D. W. Hamlyn, *A History of Western Philosophy* (London: Viking, 1987), pp. 246, 254.

15. In this sense, it might be argued that Hegel's metaphysical theory is "verifiable," or, if you prefer, "falsifiable."

16. Stepelevich, ed., *Young Hegelians*, p. 4; Toews, *Hegelianism*, pp. 141–42.

17. Schopenhauer, *The World as Will and Representation*, vol. 1, appendix: "Criticism of the Kantian Philosophy," p. 429.

18. Arthur Schopenhauer, "Fragments for the History of Philosophy," in *Parerga and Paralipomena: Short Philosophical Essays*, trans. E. F. J. Payne (Oxford: Clarendon Press, 1974), vol. 1, sec. 13, p. 96.

19. Wolfgang Schirmacher, introduction to *Arthur Schopenhauer: Philosophical Writings*, ed. Wolfgang Schirmacher, trans. Virginia Cutrufelli (New York: Continuum, 1996), p. viii.

20. See Walter Kaufmann, *Hegel: Reinterpretation, Texts and Commentary* (Garden City, NY: Doubleday, 1965), secs. 51–52.

21. See "Introduction: Translating Hegel's *Logic*," by H. S. Harris and T. F. Geraets in their translation of Hegel's *Encyclopaedia Logic*, p. xiv. The quotation within the quotation is from Alexander Pope, *An Essay on Criticism*, line 357.

22. It has recently been resurrected as a valid way of looking at history by Gordon Graham in *The Shape of the Past* (New York: Oxford University Press, 1997).

23. Karl Marx, *Capital*, trans. Samuel Moore and Edward Aveling, vol. 1, 3rd ed., in *The Marx-Engels Reader*, ed. Robert C. Tucker, 2nd ed. (New York: W. W. Norton, 1978), pp. 301, 302.

24. G. W. F. Hegel, *Reason in History*, trans. H. B. Nisbet (Cambridge: Cambridge University Press, 1975), p. 29.

25. This expression comes from Friedrich Schiller's poem "Resignation." Hegel endorses the idea of "*world history* as the *world's court of judgement*" in *Elements of the Philosophy of Right*, trans. Wood, sec. 340, p. 371 (emphasis in original).

BIBLIOGRAPHY

The following is a list of recommended readings and is not meant to be comprehensive. Books on Hegel marked * are good to begin with.

WORKS BY HEGEL IN ENGLISH TRANSLATION

Elements of the Philosophy of Right. Edited by Allen W. Wood. Translated by H. B. Nisbet. Cambridge: Cambridge University Press, 1991. (See also *Philosophy of Right,* below.)

The Encyclopaedia Logic (Encyclopaedia of the Philosophical Sciences, part 1). Translated by T. F. Geraets, W. A. Suchting, and H. S. Harris. Indianapolis: Hackett, 1991. (See also *Hegel's Logic,* below. Often referred to as "the Lesser Logic.")

The Hegel Reader. Edited by Stephen Houlgate. Oxford: Blackwell, 1998.

Hegel: Selections. Edited by M. J. Inwood. New York: Macmillan; London: Collier Macmillan, 1998.

Hegel: Texts and Commentary. Translated by Walter Kaufmann. Notre Dame, IN: University of Notre Dame Press, 1977. (Contains a fine translation of the preface to the *Phenomenology of Spirit,* with helpful explanatory notes. Also included in Kaufmann, *Hegel: Reinterpretation, Texts and Commentary,* below.)

Hegel's Logic (Encyclopaedia of the Philosophical Sciences, Part I). Translated by William Wallace. 3rd ed. Oxford: Clarendon Press, 1975. (See also *The Encyclopaedia Logic* above, which is a more recent translation of the same work. Often referred to as "the Lesser Logic.")

Hegel's Phenomenology of Spirit. Selections translated and annotated by Howard P. Kainz. University Park: Pennsylvania State University Press, 1994.

Hegel's Philosophy of Mind (*Encyclopaedia of the Philosophical Sciences*, Part III). Translated by William Wallace and A. V. Miller. Oxford: Oxford University Press, 1971.

Hegel's Philosophy of Nature (*Encyclopaedia of the Philosophical Sciences*, Part II). Translated by A. V. Miller. Oxford: Oxford University Press, 1970. (See also *Philosophy of Nature*, below, a more recent translation of the same work.)

Hegel's Political Writings. Translated by T. M. Knox. Introduction by Z. A. Pelczynski. Oxford: Oxford University Press, 1964.

Lectures on the History of Philosophy. 3 vols. Translated by E. S. Haldane and Frances H. Simson. London: Routledge and Kegan Paul; New York: Humanities Press, 1996. (See also Lauer, *Hegel's Idea of Philosophy*, below, which contains a newer translation of the introduction to this work.)

Lectures on the Philosophy of Religion. 3 vols. Edited by E. B. Speirs. Translated by Speirs and J. Burdon Sanderson. London: Routledge and Kegan Paul, 1962. (See also the next entry, a more recent, abridged translation of the same work.)

Lectures on the Philosophy of Religion. One-Volume Edition: The Lectures of 1827. Edited by Peter C. Hodgson. Translated by R. F. Brown, P. C. Hodgson, and J. M. Stewart, with assistance of H. S. Harris. Berkeley: University of California Press, 1988. (See also the previous entry.)

Lectures on the Philosophy of World History—Introduction: Reason in History. Translated by H. B. Nisbet. Cambridge: Cambridge University Press, 1975.

Phenomenology of Spirit. Translated by A. V. Miller. Oxford: Clarendon Press, 1977. (See also *Hegel: Texts and Commentary*, translated by Kaufmann, above; *Hegel's Phenomenology of Spirit*, translated by Kainz, above; O'Neill, ed., *Hegel's Dialectic of Desire and Recognition*, below; and Rauch and Sherman, *Hegel's Phenomenology of Self-Consciousness*, below. Kainz, O'Neill, and Rauch and Sherman contain newer translations of the Master and Slave section in this work.)

Philosophy of Nature. Edited and translated by M. J. Petry. 3 vols. London: Allen and Unwin; New York: Humanities Press, 1970. (See also *Hegel's Philosophy of Nature*, above.)

Philosophy of Right. Translated by T. M. Knox. Oxford: Clarendon Press, 1958. (See also *Elements of the Philosophy of Right*, above, a more recent translation of the same work.)

The Science of Logic. Translated by A. V. Miller. London: Allen and Unwin; New York: Humanities Press, 1969. (Often referred to as "the Larger Logic.")

INTRODUCTORY WORKS THAT DISCUSS HEGEL, ABSOLUTE IDEALISM, AND RELATED SUBJECTS

*Acton, H. B. "The Absolute." In *The Encyclopedia of Philosophy*, edited by Paul Edwards. New York: Macmillan and Free Press, 1967. See vol. 1, pp. 6–9.

*———. "Hegel, Georg Wilhelm Friedrich." In *The Encyclopedia of Philosophy*. Edited by Paul Edwards. New York: Macmillan and Free Press, 1967. See vol. 3, pp. 435–51.

Avineri, Shlomo. *Hegel's Theory of the Modern State*. Cambridge: Cambridge University Press, 1972.

Beiser, Frederick C., ed. *The Cambridge Companion to Hegel*. Cambridge: Cambridge University Press, 1993.

———. *Hegel*. London: Routledge, 2005.

Bernstein, Richard J. "Why Hegel Now?" *Review of Metaphysics* 31 (1977–78): 29–60.

*Brown, Alison Leigh. *On Hegel*. Belmont, CA: Wadsworth, 2001.

Burbidge, John. "Hegel's Absolutes." *Owl of Minerva* 29 (1997): 23–37.

———. *Historical Dictionary of Hegelian Philosophy*. Lanham, MD: Scarecrow Press, 2001.

Butler, Clark. *Hegel*. Boston: Twayne, 1977.

*Caird, Edward. *Hegel*. Edinburgh: William Blackwood and Sons, 1883; North Haven, CT: Archon Books, 1968; Whitefish, MT: Kessinger Publishing, 2004.

*Copleston, F. J. *A History of Philosophy, Vol. 7—Modern Philosophy, Part I: Fichte to Hegel*. Garden City, NY: Image Books, 1963.

*Critchley, Simon. *Continental Philosophy: A Very Short Introduction*. New York: Oxford University Press, 2001.

Crites, Stephen D. "Hegelianism." In *The Encyclopedia of Philosophy*, edited by Paul Edwards. New York: Macmillan and Free Press, 1967. See vol. 3, pp. 451–58.

Fackenheim, Emil L., and James A. Doull. "Would Hegel Today Be a Hegelian?" *Dialogue* 9 (1970): 222–35.

Feibleman, James K. "Hegel Revisited." In *Studies in Hegel*. New Orleans: Tulane University; The Hague: Martinus Nijhoff, 1960. See pp. 16–49.

Findlay, J. N. "The Contemporary Relevance of Hegel." In *Hegel: A Collection of Critical Essays*, edited by Alasdair MacIntyre. Garden City, NY: Doubleday, 1972. See pp. 1–20.

*———. *Hegel: A Re-examination*. New York: Collier Books, 1962. (Reprinted New York: Ashgate Press, 1993.)

Harris, Errol. "Introduction: The Contemporary Relevance of Hegel's Philosophy" and "Absolute Spirit in History." In *The Spirit of Hegel*, by Errol Harris. Atlantic Highlands, NJ: Humanities Press, 1993. See pp. 1–19, 208–22.

Harris, H. S. "The Legacy of Hegel." *Monist* 48 (1964): 112–32.
*Heiss, Robert. *Hegel, Kierkegaard, Marx: Three Great Philosophers Whose Ideas Changed the Course of Civilization.* Translated by E. B. Garside. New York: Dell, 1975. Part 1: "Hegel's Dialectical System."
*Horstmann, Rolf-Peter. "Hegel, Georg Wilhelm Friedrich (1770–1831)." In *Routledge Encyclopedia of Philosophy,* edited by Edward Craig. London and New York: Routledge, 1998. See vol. 4, pp. 259–80.
———. "What Is Hegel's Legacy and What Should We Do With It?" *European Journal of Philosophy* 7 (1999): 275–87.
*Houlgate, Stephen. *Freedom, Truth and History: An Introduction to Hegel's Philosophy.* London: Routledge, 1991.
*———. "G. W. F. Hegel." In *The Blackwell Guide to the Modern Philosophers from Descartes to Nietzsche,* edited by Steven Emmanuel. Cambridge, MA: Blackwell, 2000, see pp. 278–305.
———. "G. W. F. Hegel: The *Phenomenology of Spirit.*" In *Blackwell Guide to Contemporary Philosophy,* edited by Robert C. Solomon. Malden, MA: Blackwell, 2003, see pp. 8–29.
———. "G. W. F. Hegel, *Phenomenology of Spirit* (1807): Thinking Philosophically without Begging the Question." In *The Classics of Western Philosophy: A Reader's Guide,* edited by J. E. Jorge. Malden, MA: Blackwell, 2003, see pp. 364–82.
*Inwood, Michael J. "Hegel." In *The Blackwell Companion to Philosophy,* edited by B. F. Bunnin. Cambridge, MA: Blackwell, 1996, see chap. 23.
*Jones, W. T. *A History of Western Philosophy.* 3rd ed. Fort Worth, TX: Harcourt Brace College Publishers, 1997.
Kaufmann, Walter. *Hegel: Reinterpretation, Texts and Commentary.* Garden City, NY: Doubleday, 1965; Notre Dame, IN: University of Notre Dame Press, 1977.
———, ed. *Hegel's Political Philosophy.* New York: Atherton Press, 1970.
*Kenny, Anthony. *A Brief History of Western Philosophy.* Cambridge, MA: Blackwell, 1998.
Knowles, Dudley. *Routledge Philosophy Guidebook to Hegel and the "Philosophy of Right."* London and New York: Routledge, 2002.
*Lauer, Quentin. *Hegel's Idea of Philosophy.* New York: Fordham University Press, 1971.
*Lavine, T. Z. *From Socrates to Sartre: The Philosophic Quest.* Part 4, "Hegel." Toronto: Bantam Books, 1984.
Loewith, Karl. *From Hegel to Nietzsche: The Revolution in Nineteenth-Century Thought.* Translated by David E. Green. New York: Holt, Rinehart and Winston, 1964.
MacIntyre, Alasdair, ed. *Hegel: A Collection of Critical Essays.* Garden City, NY: Doubleday Anchor Books, 1972.

Marcuse, Herbert. *Reason and Revolution: Hegel and the Rise of Social Theory.* Boston: Beacon Press, 1960.

*Matson, Wallace. *A New History of Philosophy.* Vol. 2, *From Descartes to Searle.* Fort Worth, TX: Harcourt College Publishers, 2000.

McCarney, Joseph. *Routledge Philosophy Guidebook to Hegel on History.* London and New York: Routledge, 2000.

Merleau-Ponty, Maurice. "Hegel's Existentialism." In *Sense and Non-Sense,* translated by Hubert L. Dreyfus and Patricia Allen Dreyfus. Evanston, IL: Northwestern University Press, 1964. See pp. 63–70.

*Mure, G. R. G. *The Philosophy of Hegel.* London: Oxford University Press, 1965.

Norman, Richard. *Hegel's "Phenomenology": A Philosophical Introduction.* Brighton, UK: Sussex University Press; Toronto: Clarke, Irwin, 1976.

O'Brien, George Dennis. *Hegel on Reason and History: A Contemporary Introduction.* Chicago: University of Chicago Press, 1975.

Pinkard, Terry. *German Philosophy 1760–1860: The Legacy of Idealism.* Cambridge: Cambridge University Press, 2002.

*Plant, Raymond. *Hegel.* London: Phoenix Press, 1997; New York: Routledge, 1999.

*Rockmore, Tom. *Before and after Hegel: An Historical Introduction to Hegel's Thought.* Berkeley: University of California Press, 1993; Indianapolis: Hackett, 2003.

*Royce, Josiah. *Lectures on Modern Idealism.* New Haven, CT: Yale University Press, 1919.

*Schacht, Richard. *Hegel and After: Studies in Continental Philosophy between Kant and Sartre.* Pittsburgh: University of Pittsburgh Press, 1975.

Schroeder, William Ralph. "Hegel." In *Sartre and His Predecessors: The Self and the Other.* London: Routledge and Kegan Paul, 1984.

Siep, Ludwig. "Individuality in Hegel's *Phenomenology of Spirit.*" In *The Modern Subject: Conceptions of the Self in Classical German Philosophy,* edited by Karl Ameriks and Dieter Sturma. Albany: State University of New York Press, 1995. See pp. 131–47.

*Singer, Peter. *Hegel: A Very Short Introduction.* New York: Oxford University Press, 2001.

Solomon, Robert C. *From Hegel to Existentialism.* New York: Oxford University Press, 1987.

———. *Routledge History of Philosophy.* Vol. 6, *The Age of German Idealism.* London: Routledge, 1993.

*Solomon, Robert C., and Kathleen M. Higgins, eds. *A Passion for Wisdom: A Very Short History of Philosophy.* New York: Oxford University Press, 1997.

Stern, Robert. *Routledge Philosophy Guidebook to Hegel and the "Phenomenology of Spirit."* London and New York: Routledge, 2002.

Stern, Robert, and Nicholas Walker. "Hegelianism." In *Routledge Encyclopedia of*

Philosophy, edited by Edward Craig. London and New York: Routledge, 1998. See vol. 4, pp. 280–302.

*Stumpf, Samuel Enoch, and James Fieser. *Socrates to Sartre and Beyond: A History of Philosophy*. 7th ed. New York: McGraw-Hill, 2002.

*Taylor, Charles. *Hegel*. Cambridge: Cambridge University Press, 1975.

*———. *Hegel and Modern Society*. Cambridge: Cambridge University Press, 1979.

*Teichman, Jenny, and Graham White, eds. *An Introduction to Modern European Philosophy*. New York: St. Martin's Press, 1995.

Westphal, Kenneth R. *Hegel's Epistemology: A Philosophical Introduction to the "Phenomenology of Spirit."* Indianapolis: Hackett, 2003.

MORE ADVANCED WORKS THAT DISCUSS HEGEL, ABSOLUTE IDEALISM, AND RELATED SUBJECTS

Collins, Ardis, ed. *Hegel and the Modern World*. Albany: State University of New York Press, 1995.

Craig, Edward. *The Mind of God and the Works of Man*. Oxford: Clarendon Press, 1996.

Dahlstrom, Daniel. "Hegel's Questionable Legacy." *Research in Phenomenology* 32 (2002): 3–25.

Dallmayr, Fred R. *G. W. F. Hegel: Modernity and Politics*. Lanham, MD: Rowman and Littlefield, 2002.

Denker, Alfred, and Michael Vater, eds. *Hegel's "Phenomenology of Spirit": New Critical Essays*. Amherst, NY: Humanity Books, 2003.

Dienstag, Joshua Foa. "What Is Living and What Is Dead in the Interpretation of Hegel?" *Political Theory* 29 (2001): 262–75.

Duquette, David A. *Hegel's History of Philosophy: New Interpretations*. Albany: State University of New York Press, 2002.

Englehardt, H. Tristram, Jr. *Hegel Reconsidered*. Dordrecht: Kluwer, 1994.

Fackenheim, Emil L. *The Religious Dimension in Hegel's Thought*. Bloomington: Indiana University Press, 1967.

Forster, Michael N. *Hegel and Skepticism*. Cambridge, MA: Harvard University Press, 1989.

Franco, Paul. *Hegel's Philosophy of Freedom*. New Haven, CT: Yale University Press, 1999.

Gadamer, Hans-Georg. *Hegel's Dialectic: Five Hermeneutical Studies*. Translated by P. C. Smith. New Haven, CT: Yale University Press, 1976.

Graham, Gordon. *The Shape of the Past*. New York: Oxford University Press, 1997.

Halper, Edward. "Hegel's Family Values." *Review of Metaphysics* 54 (2001): 815–58.

Hampsher-Monk, Iain. *A History of Modern Political Thought: Major Political Thinkers from Hobbes to Marx.* Cambridge, MA: Blackwell, 1993.

Hardimon, Michael O. *Hegel's Social Philosophy: The Project of Reconciliation.* New York: Cambridge University Press, 1994.

———. "The Project of Reconciliation: Hegel's Social Philosophy." *Philosophy and Public Affairs* 21 (1992): 165–95.

Herbert, Gary B. *A Philosophical History of Rights.* New Brunswick, NJ: Transaction Publishers, 2002.

Höffe, Otfried, and Robert B. Pippin, eds. *Hegel on Ethics and Politics.* Cambridge: Cambridge University Press, 2004.

Houlgate, Stephen. *Hegel, Nietzsche and the Criticism of Metaphysics.* Cambridge: Cambridge University Press, 1986.

Hutchings, Kimberly. *Hegel: A Feminist Revision.* Cambridge, UK: Polity Press, 2003.

Inwood, Michael J. *Hegel.* London: Routledge, 2002.

———. *A Hegel Dictionary.* Oxford: Blackwell, 1992.

———, ed. *Hegel.* Oxford: Oxford University Press, 1985.

Kain, Philip J. *Hegel and the Other: A Study of the "Phenomenology of Spirit."* Albany: State University of New York Press, 2005.

———. "Hegel, Reason, and Idealism." *Idealistic Studies* 27 (1997): 97–112.

Kainz, Howard P. *G. W. F. Hegel: The Philosophical System.* Boston: Twayne; London: Prentice Hall International, 1996.

———. *Hegel's "Phenomenology, Part I": Analysis and Commentary.* Tuscaloosa: University of Alabama Press, 1976.

———. *Hegel's "Phenomenology, Part II": The Evolution of Ethical and Religious Consciousness to the Absolute Standpoint.* Athens: University of Ohio Press, 1983.

Lamb, D. *Hegel: From Foundation to System.* The Hague: Martinus Nijhoff, 1980.

Lauer, Quentin. *A Reading of Hegel's "Phenomenology of Spirit."* 2nd ed. New York: Fordham University Press, 1993.

Levenson, Carl A., and Jonathan Westphal, eds. *Reality.* Indianapolis: Hackett, 1994.

Levin, Jerome D. *Theories of the Self.* Washington, DC: Taylor-Francis, 1992.

Longuenesse, Béatrice. *Hegel's Critique of Metaphysics.* Cambridge: Cambridge University Press, 2006.

Lukács, György. *Young Hegel.* Translated by Rodney Livingstone. Cambridge, MA: MIT Press, 1976.

Maker, William. *Philosophy without Foundations: Rethinking Hegel.* Albany: State University of New York Press, 1994.

McCabe, David. "Hegel and the Idea of Philosophical History." *History of Philosophy Quarterly* 15 (1998): 369–88.

McRae, Robert Grant. *Philosophy and the Absolute: The Modes of Hegel's Speculation.* Dordrecht: Martinus Nijhoff; Hingham, MA: Kluwer, 1985.

Mills, Patricia Jagentowicz, ed. *Feminist Interpretations of G. W. F. Hegel.* University Park: Pennsylvania State University Press, 1996.

Nancy, Jean-Luc. *Hegel: The Restlessness of the Negative.* Translated by Jason Smith and Steven Miller. Minneapolis: University of Minnesota Press, 2002.

Neuhouser, F. *Foundations of Hegel's Social Theory: Actualizing Freedom.* Cambridge, MA: Harvard University Press, 2000.

Norman, Richard J. *Hegel, Marx and Dialectic: A Debate.* Brighton, UK: Harvester Press; Atlantic Highlands, NJ: Humanities Press, 1980.

O'Neill, John, ed. *Hegel's Dialectic of Desire and Recognition: Texts and Commentary.* Albany: State University of New York Press, 1996.

Ormiston, Alice. *Love and Politics: Re-Interpreting Hegel.* Albany: State University of New York Press, 2004.

Pelczynski, Z. A., ed. *Hegel's Political Philosophy: Problems and Perspectives.* Cambridge: Cambridge University Press, 1971.

———, ed. *The State and Civil Society: Studies in Hegel's Political Philosophy.* Cambridge: Cambridge University Press, 1984.

Peperzak, Adriaan Theodoor. *Modern Freedom: Hegel's Legal, Moral, and Political Philosophy.* Dordrecht: Kluwer, 2001.

———, ed. *Philosophy and Politics: A Commentary on the Preface to Hegel's "Philosophy of Right."* Dordrecht: Kluwer, 2002.

Pippin, Robert B. "Hegel and Institutional Rationality." *Southern Journal of Philosophy,* suppl. vol. 39 (2001): 1–25.

———. "Hegel's Original Insight." *International Philosophical Quarterly* 33 (1993): 285–96.

———. "What Is the Problem for Which Hegel's Theory of Recognition Is the Answer?" *European Journal of Philosophy* 8 (2000): 155–72.

Priest, Stephen, ed. *Hegel's Critique of Kant.* Oxford: Clarendon Press, 1987.

Quante, Michael. *Hegel's Concept of Action.* Cambridge: Cambridge University Press, 2004.

Rauch, Leo, and David Sherman. *Hegel's Phenomenology of Self-Consciousness: Text and Commentary.* Albany: State University of New York Press, 1999.

Rockmore, Tom. *Hegel's Circular Epistemology.* Bloomington: Indiana University Press, 1986.

———. On Hegel's *"Epistemology and Contemporary Philosophy."* Atlantic Highlands, NJ: Humanities Press, 1996.

Schmidt, Dennis J. "Why Is Spirit Such a Slow Learner?" *Research in Phenomenology* 32 (2002): 26–43.

Sedgwick, Sally. "The State as Organism: The Metaphysical Basis of Hegel's *Philosophy of Right.*" *Southern Journal of Philosophy,* suppl. vol. 39 (2001): 171–88.

Shklar, Judith N. *Freedom and Independence: A Study of the Political Ideas of Hegel's "Phenomenology of Mind."* Cambridge: Cambridge University Press, 1976.

Singh, R. P. "Contradiction and Sublation: Hegel's Dialectic." *Indian Philosophical Quarterly* (1991): 501–18.

Smith, Kenneth. "Two Concepts of Spirit in Hegel." *Southwestern Philosophical Studies* 14 (1992): 98–110.

Sprigge, T. L. S. *The Vindication of Absolute Idealism.* Edinburgh: Edinburgh University Press, 1983.

Steinkraus, Warren, ed. *Studies in Hegel's Philosophy.* New York: Holt, Rinehart and Winston, 1971.

Stepelevich, Lawrence S., ed. *Selected Essays on G. W. F. Hegel.* Atlantic Highlands, NJ: Humanities Press, 1994.

Stern, R. *Georg Wilhelm Friedrich Hegel: Critical Assessments.* 4 vols. London: Routledge, 1993.

Stewart, Jon. *The Hegel Myths and Legends.* Evanston, IL: Northwestern University Press, 1996.

———. "Hegel and the Myth of Reason." *Owl of Minerva* 26 (1995): 187–200.

———. *Kierkegaard's Relations to Hegel Reconsidered.* Cambridge: Cambridge University Press, 2003.

Taylor, Mark C. *Journeys to Selfhood: Hegel and Kierkegaard.* Berkeley: University of California Press, 1980.

Toews, John Edward. *Hegelianism: The Path toward Dialectical Humanism, 1805–1841.* Cambridge: Cambridge University Press, 1980.

Tunick, M. *Hegel's Political Philosophy.* Princeton, NJ: Princeton University Press, 1992.

White, A. *Absolute Knowledge: Hegel and the Problem of Metaphysics.* Athens: Ohio University Press, 1983.

Wilkinson, James H. "On Hegel's Project." *British Journal for the History of Philosophy* 2 (1994): 87–144.

Williams, Robert R. *Hegel's Ethics of Recognition.* Berkeley: University of California Press, 1997.

———, ed. *Beyond Liberalism and Communitarianism: Studies in Hegel's "Philosophy of Right."* Albany: State University of New York Press, 2001.

Wisdom, J. O. "What Was Hegel's Main Problem?" *Philosophy of the Social Sciences* 23 (1993): 411–24.

Wood, Allen W. *Hegel's Ethical Thought.* Cambridge: Cambridge University Press, 1990.

MAINLY BIOGRAPHICAL WORKS ON HEGEL

Althaus, Horst. *Hegel: An Intellectual Biography.* Translated by Michael Tarsh. Cambridge, UK: Polity Press; Malden, MA: Blackwell, 2000.

Butler, Clark, and Christiane Seiler, trans. *Hegel: The Letters.* Bloomington: Indiana University Press, 1984.

Pinkard, Terry. *Hegel: A Biography.* Cambridge: Cambridge University Press, 2000.

*Wiedman, Franz. *Hegel: An Illustrated Biography.* Translated by Joachim Neugroschel. New York: Pegasus, 1968.

INTERNET RESOURCES FOR INFORMATION ON HEGEL

(All items marked † can be reached via any search engine by the following route: Society for German Idealism (www.lclark.edu/~idealism/ SGI.html)—links—Hegel Society of America—Hegel Links Throughout the Internet.)

†Blunden, Andy. "Hegel by HyperText." http://marxists.org/reference/archive/ hegel/.

†Chitty, A. E. "A Hegel Bibliography." www.sussex.ac.uk/Users/sefd0/bib/ hegel.htm.

Duquette, David. "Hegel: Social and Political Thought." *Internet Encyclopedia of Philosophy,* editor James Fraser; assistant general editor Bradley Dowden. www.iep.utm.edu/.

†Froeb, Kai. Hegel.net. Links can be followed from this Web site to other useful Hegel Web sites. www.hegel.net.

†Hegel Society of America. Links can be followed from this Web site to other useful Hegel Web sites. www.hegel.org.

"Introduction to Hegel's Philosophy." An introductory course on Hegel (for members only). (See also Yahoo Groups, below.) http://groups.yahoo .com/group/intro_hegel/.

†Marchetti, Mike. gwfhegel.org. Links can be followed from this Web site to other useful Hegel Web sites. www.gwfhegel.org.

†Mickelsen, Carl. "Carl Mickelsen's Hegel Site." www.class.uidaho.edu/ mickelsen/hegel1310.htm.

Philosophy Research Base. Featured Webs include: Nineteenth Century Philosophy; Browse Philosophical Topics; Browse Philosophers; Browse History of Philosophy. www.erraticimpact.com/.

Questia. The Online Library of Books and Journals. Hegel texts and works on Hegel available for reading. www.questia.com.

Redding, Paul. "G. W. F. Hegel." *Stanford Encyclopedia of Philosophy (Summer 2002 Edition),* ed. Edward N. Zalta. http://plato.stanford.edu/archives/ sum2000/entries/hegel.

Yahoo Groups. Search "Hegel": here you can enter discussions of specific topics in Hegelian studies or become a member of a certain group. http://groups .yahoo.com/.

INDEX